Praise for *Never Outmatched*

"Lee Pepper turns a lifetime of high-performance leadership in the military and marketing into a 'yes you can do' handbook for winning your marketing wars. Simply put, read *Never Outmatched*; you're in the hands of a master."
~NOAH BENSHEA, International Bestselling Author and Advisor

"*Never Outmatched* is more than a business book—it's a tactical masterclass in leadership. Lee Pepper distills battlefield wisdom into sharp, actionable strategies that every modern marketer and executive needs. If you want to lead with courage, clarity, and command, this is your playbook."
~JOHN WEST, cofounder of The Guest House Ocala

"Starting, operating, and maintaining a business is a difficult and daunting task. Everywhere we look, we are bombarded with strategy and advice from 'know-it-alls' and bad actors. The pages of *Never Outmatched* contains ancient wisdom, modern ingenuity, and counter-intuitive pragmatism. This book provides simple, yet comprehensive tools for navigating and overcoming the challenges and complexity of business in the modern world; a guide for kicking ass in the twenty-first century."
~DAVE SMITH, mindfulness and emotional intelligence trainer, dharma teacher, author and musician

"Lee Pepper bridges the gap between battlefield strategy and business results like no one else. *Never Outmatched* is a concise, powerful guide packed with wisdom from his unique experience as an army officer and a marketing executive—essential reading for any leader determined to win."
> ~HOWARD MILLER, professor of history at Lipscomb University

"I've known Lee Pepper since his days leading marketing for one of the top treatment centers in the country where his campaigns were so effective, they had to keep opening new facilities just to meet demand. In *Never Outmatched*, he combines military precision with real-world marketing know-how to give entrepreneurs a true strategic edge. This book is a powerful, practical guide for anyone serious about winning in business."
> ~KEN SEELEY, author, interventionist on *A&E*, founder of Intervention 911

"As the world has transformed from an agrarian based economy to the dawn of a knowledge-based economy, one institution in every country has had to adapt, if not lead, those transformations: the military. Lee Pepper's book *Never Outmatched* will provide you with insights and real-life examples of how you can apply the lessons the military over time. Get insight on how to constantly assess your situation and adapt to circumstances beyond your control with a team that can manage change without missing a beat."
> ~RUSSELL VERNEY, campaign manager and consultant for Ross Perot's 1992 and 1996 presidential campaigns, regional director for Judicial Watch

"The battlefield is a masterclass in innovation, and Lee Pepper is a seasoned commander who's turned those lessons into market victories. *Never Outmatched* is your battle plan for taking the offensive in business, not just surviving but dominating. The rules have changed—don't show up to a modern business war with a pistol and a playbook from the past."
~NIGEL GREEN, coach to high-performing CEOs and architect of Scalable Sales Systems

NEVER OUTMATCHED

★ ★ ★ ★ ★ ★ ★ ★ ★ ★ ★ ★

MILITARY STRATEGIES
——— TO ———
LEAD, INNOVATE, AND WIN IN THE

MODERN MARKETING BATTLEFIELD

LEE PEPPER

Forefront
BOOKS

Never Outmatched: Military Strategies to Lead, Innovate, and
Win in the Modern Marketing Battlefield

Copyright © 2025 by Lee Pepper

All rights reserved. No part of this publication may be reproduced, stored in a retrieval system, or transmitted in any form by any means, electronic, mechanical, photocopy, recording, or otherwise, without the prior permission of the publisher, except as provided by USA copyright law.

No patent liability is assumed with respect to the use of the information contained herein. Although every precaution has been taken in the preparation of this book, the publisher and author assume no responsibility for errors or omissions. Neither is any liability assumed for damages resulting from the use of the information contained herein.

Published by Mission Driven Press, an imprint of Forefront Books.
Distributed by Simon & Schuster.

Library of Congress Control Number: 2025910411

Print ISBN: 978-1-63763-461-5
E-book ISBN: 978-1-63763-462-2

Cover Design by George Stevens, G Sharp Design LLC
Interior Design by Bill Kersey, KerseyGraphics

Printed in the United States of America

25 26 27 28 29 30 [RR4] 10 9 8 7 6 5 4 3 2 1

DEDICATION

First and foremost, to my amazing wife, Jennifer, whose unbridled creativity in the studio and connection with her students sets an example for me to aspire to. Anytime I was facing a challenge, she was the first to reassure me that I was not crazy!

To my sons, Miles and Cy, who bring great joy, humor, and meaning to my life. I'm glad you all are always up for adventures big and small. No matter if we were going by foot, bicycle, or car, I've always had a smile knowing you were near.

To my family who served, Bruce A. "Pete" Pepper Jr., Tom Whayne, Todd Pepper, Bruce A. Pepper Sr., Gordon Hacker, Brents Pepper, Adam Pepper, Ronald Pepper, Wood E. "Bud" Currens, Ian Smith, and Jack Fiaschetti.

Finally, to my namesake, Leander Pepper, who fell at the Battle of Shiloh in the spring of 1862.

CONTENTS

Preface 11
Introduction 17
Chapter 1: Outnumbered but Never Outmatched 21
Chapter 2: Commander's Intent 41
Chapter 3: Citizen Farmer, Citizen Soldier 61
Chapter 4: Force Multiplication 79
Chapter 5: War-Gaming 103
Chapter 6: Anvil and Hammer 125
Chapter 7: Intelligence 145
Chapter 8: Counterinsurgency 165
Chapter 9: Working with Allies 185
Chapter 10: Circumvallation 195
Chapter 11: Operational Readiness 213
Chapter 12: Combat Organization 231
Afterword: Be Action-Oriented Today 251
Acknowledgments 253
About the Author 259
Notes 261

PREFACE

The genesis of this book was coming into focus as my time at Foundations Recovery Network (FRN) started producing results and gaining recognition. Our private equity sponsor at that time, Sterling Partners, invited me to present at a marketing meeting of portfolio companies in Chicago. All our sister companies from different verticals would be there.

I went to work with my team in Nashville, crafting a presentation to showcase our digital work. I decided to forgo the traditional PowerPoint presentation and record my presentation as a YouTube video. My presentation featured my team covering their areas of expertise, all wrapped up in six minutes. Cherie Carter shared SEO tips, Anna McKenzie spoke about authoritative content, Zander Jones shared our case study about engagement through National Recovery Month, and even our intern, Chelsea Gunn, shared our social media calendar approach. These pieces were masterfully packaged in video format by our world-class videographer, Caleb McLaughlin. I planned to be onstage to start the video and then be available for questions. It seems basic now, but this was cutting edge in 2010.

As we were finishing the video presentation a couple of weeks before the event, the coordinators in Chicago began to push back on my delivery method. "We've never done it that way," they argued. They insisted I share a PowerPoint deck and read my slides from the lectern in person. I resisted, and the escalation started.

Our CEO advised me to deliver it as they wanted. I stood my ground. I wasn't trying to be difficult, really. My position was that marketing had changed. Digital marketing had upset the apple cart, so to speak, and the traditional methods were no longer as effective as they used to be. I was the chief information officer at the time, not even the chief marketing officer. Digital marketing still lived in the world of chief information and technology officers.

My presentation as a video and the inclusion of the people who made our approach work was fundamental. Our sister portfolio companies were in danger of falling behind as new platforms and marketing approaches emerged. They were not even aware of the new staffing model required to compete. Any deviation from the presentation I envisioned would not deliver the impact the partners wanted me to share.

PREFACE

As we approached the meeting date, they gave in. Was it risky? I don't think so. I love the quote often attributed (debatably) to Alexander Hamilton: "If you stand for nothing, you'll fall for anything."

In the military and early in my career with Ross Perot, I was encouraged to be creative, take initiative, and challenge conventional thinking. I believed the decision-makers wanted to see my real presentation. It was just the middle-layer bureaucracy that was getting in the way.

I was right about the audience's response to the video format. They loved it.

In fact, this prerecorded video keynote format has recently become the default method for Apple to deliver its highly publicized product announcements. For decades, Apple's keynote presentations—especially when headlined in person by Steve Jobs—were the gold standard of corporate presentations. During COVID, however, Apple ended their live stage presentations and pivoted to prefilmed, fully edited presentations. Though they faced some early criticism, they've kept this format in place post-COVID, and Apple fans have accepted it as the norm.

Shortly after that presentation, I was invited to visit other portfolio companies to share how they could take advantage of the growing digital marketing landscape.

Within the year, our CEO promoted me to chief marketing officer in addition to CIO. The thought

PREFACE

process in developing that initial presentation and its successful reception encouraged me to soldier on in my approach to marketing and keep notes over the years.

Those notes turned into other presentations and eventually into an early draft manuscript of this book. I started sharing these mental models in leadership meetings and boardrooms, explaining my marketing strategy through the lens of strategic military thinking. All of a sudden, innovative, cutting-edge approaches to marketing that would typically be dismissed as fads were now understood. Executives' faces would light up, and we now had the moment to unleash the creative forces and build momentum aligned with our business and supported by our leadership.

I started keeping a spreadsheet a year before I began working with my editor, tracking my daily word count to hold myself accountable for writing and research. Based on conversations with authors Rory and AJ Vaden (founders of Brand Builders Group), I had in my head that I needed fifty thousand words.

I was sitting at thirty thousand words when I caught up with Nigel Green on a phone call. I had recruited him to revamp our business development team at FRN to great success, and he published a book on sales and business development titled *Revenue Harvest*. He flat out told me it was time to engage an editor; I had enough to move this project

PREFACE

into overdrive. He introduced me to the esteemed Liam Curley.

Liam is a UK-based content strategist. Over seven months, he helped guide me through his process of restructuring my writing into the mental models I deliver in this book. From my first Google Meet with him across the pond, I knew that the essence of my writing consisted of the mental models these military strategies represented.

Why do you need to understand these mental models?

I've arrived at companies in turnaround and start-up modes or been hired to help the business expand into new markets. All had a similar problem: Their perception of "marketing" or their "marketing leader" was not working. There's a good chance you are going to face a similar crisis at some point.

As Mike Tyson famously said, "Everyone has a plan until they get punched in the mouth."

Building your marketing and leadership plans around these mental models inspired by military strategy will unite you and your team but also neatly align you with your C-suite peers.

In today's volunteer military, less than 1 percent of our citizens serve in the armed forces. That means many great people working in business today have never been exposed to these approaches. I wrote this

PREFACE

book to share these ideas, which have served previous generations and me so well.

I have included actionable suggestions throughout this book, and you will read the stories and figure out how to implement similar strategies in your business or career. But the real win for you will be understanding the bigger picture of what these military-inspired strategies can deliver to your view of marketing, your approach to your business, and the teams that run your business. Determine today that in the face of adversity, you will never be outmatched.

INTRODUCTION

I loved giving tours of our marketing teams at Foundations Recovery Network (Foundations), SpecialtyCare, and The Meadows. It was a chance to network in our industries, develop allies for our marketing efforts, and hopefully learn some new things from the people who came through.

"I cannot get approval to do this." I heard this refrain often on our tours.

"I did not seek approval to build this," I would always reply.

Barriers are everywhere—some real, some imagined. Both can keep you from achieving your potential. Both can be overcome.

---- ★ ----

Opportunities don't happen. You create them.
—*Chris Grosser*[1]

---- ★ ----

INTRODUCTION

Approval is an interesting concept. We get hired or promoted to do a job or execute a mission, but we can quickly fall into a pattern of seeking approval to do our job or to lead our mission. All of a sudden, your boss is doing your job along with their job, and you wonder why things are not moving quickly. You feel stuck, thinking, *Why won't they approve so I can start doing my job?*

I'm not suggesting you act outside of budget, scope, or good governance. My point is that you have a lot more room to maneuver than you are giving yourself credit for. I have yet to see a budget or staff that cannot be realigned creatively in order to demonstrate one's marketing capability, which will then lead to success and more room to grow.

As we built Foundations Recovery Network, a leading provider of addiction and mental health treatment, we were able to provide a sixtyfold return to our investors. That was not always done with a larger budget and more spending. When I arrived, I inherited a budget heavy on Yellow Pages and television spending. I wasn't hired to manage the status quo; I was hired to scale our marketing to the potential our investors believed in.

You were not hired to maintain the status quo either. Even if you are in a wildly successful business, disruption will arrive on your doorstep at some point.

INTRODUCTION

Your Ability to Communicate Your Vision Is Critical

The vision you share needs to be easily discernible through mental models. Many of your leadership peers will come from different disciplines. Marketing is often viewed as a black box, something mysterious to be divined rather than empirically determined. Or it is perceived as something easily accomplished or not sophisticated.

The mental models I use in this book derive from successful military strategies I've applied to marketing. Some of these strategies are centuries old and have undergone numerous iterations as technology and science have evolved.

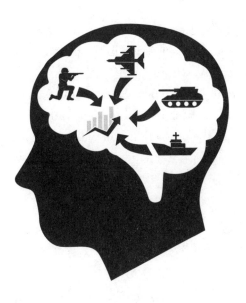

INTRODUCTION

Applying these models will arm you in new ways for corporate battle. These strategies can be applied to connect your creative vision to the material impact your team can have on the business.

We are not facing a life-or-death decision, but we and our companies are facing a success-or-failure situation.

---- ★ ----

Inaction breeds doubt and fear. Action breeds confidence and courage. If you want to conquer fear, do not sit home and think about it. Go out and get busy.
—Dale Carnegie[2]

---- ★ ----

The applications can be profound for you, uniting your team and your C-suite in the pursuit of excellence and, ultimately, winning.

You don't have to be a veteran of the armed services to understand these mental models, but you do have to subscribe to the ethos that you will *never be outmatched*.

Chapter 1

OUTNUMBERED BUT NEVER OUTMATCHED

The staff sergeant riding with us atop our M1 Abrams battle tank at Fort Knox would regularly bark, "What are you going to do now, Lieutenant? Five, four, three, two, ..."

———— ★ ————

Armor soldiers and cavalry troopers must thrive in conditions of ambiguity and uncertainty, seeking opportunities to seize, retain, and exploit the initiative with the goal of preserving freedom of action for friendly forces while denying options to the enemy.
—Lt. Gen. Kevin D. Admiral[3]

———— ★ ————

Men and women rarely come to the army instinctively knowing what it means to think and act quickly.

It requires tutelage to complete the transformation into warriors and leaders and to instill the skill and drive required for success.

I spent ten years as CIO and CMO at Foundations Recovery Network (Foundations). When I left, we had grown our shareholder value sixtyfold across two private equity owners and successfully sold for $350 million, a record valuation at the time. My approach to leading at those levels was rooted in the fundamental military strategies I learned during my service in the United States Army.

I learned early on that I would never have everything perfect in the army, and decisions cannot wait for ideal scenarios. The weather would not always cooperate, the terrain would not always be advantageous, staffing shortages could pop up, the supply of munitions and food could be delayed or disrupted, and communications up and down the chain of command could be interrupted.

--- ★ ---

War is the realm of uncertainty; three quarters of the factors on which action is based are wrapped in a fog of greater or lesser uncertainty. A sensitive and discriminating judgment is called for; a skilled intelligence to scent out the truth.
—Carl von Clausewitz[4]

--- ★ ---

When I started working in the corporate world, things were not perfect either. Recruiting talent for my teams would take longer than expected, new product or feature launches would be delayed, the scope of projects could creep and expand, the budget could be cut or reallocated, equipment deliveries could be delayed, new and unexpected competitors would arrive, phone systems would crash, servers would overheat, and office space would be short.

I spent many hours reading Carl von Clausewitz's writings in Armor School at Fort Knox, Kentucky, and was especially influenced by his commentaries on the inherent uncertainties in military endeavors and the need to act decisively despite imperfect circumstances. Clausewitz frequently advocated for boldness and calculating risk rather than waiting for perfect conditions, which often leads to inaction and missed opportunities.

I determined that even when faced with all the challenges a leader faces, I was never going to be outmatched. I would employ the fundamental strategies I learned in the service that were now core to my approach to leadership.

Leading Fewer Troops to Greater Victories

Almost a year after the Imperial Japanese Navy Air Service attack on Pearl Harbor, Allied forces sought to open a second front against the Axis powers. Looking at the world map and the number of battles lost, it appeared the United States and its allies were outnumbered. The US-led plan to turn the tide started with Operation Torch, in which the Allied forces would land in three groups in the Vichy French–controlled North Africa.

After the initial landings in Morocco and Algeria, the Allies created defenses in the Tunisian Dorsal, an extension of the Atlas Mountains. Maj. Gen. Lloyd Fredendall commanded the US II Corps during the landings and was set to face off with the Axis powers. The Kasserine Pass was a critical gap in the Dorsal. German general Erwin Rommel sought to use his vaunted Afrika Corps to surprise the American and British forces in late February 1943.

The Americans' inexperience, poor leadership, and inadequate training led to ten thousand casualties inflicted by Rommel's troops. Numerous tanks and vehicles were also destroyed or captured, and Allied morale suffered a severe blow after this high-profile defeat.

Fredendall had served in various roles in the years preceding the invasion of North Africa, primarily due to his administrative skills. During the Kasserine Pass failure, Fredendall was criticized for micromanaging his subordinates and dispersing his units over a wide area, which prevented them from combining their strength and left them open to attack. He was also taken to task for rarely visiting the front lines and commanding from a fortified bunker at a distance. This led Gen. Dwight Eisenhower to transform Fredendall's II Corps significantly.

In the midst of chaos, there is also opportunity.
—*Sun Tzu*[5]

Within days of the disastrous loss at the Kasserine Pass, Gen. George S. Patton was appointed the new commander of the US II Corps. Patton was chosen to take over because of his exceptional leadership qualities and reputation for operating with order and discipline. Eisenhower, the Supreme Allied Commander, knew he needed a leader with the charisma to restore American morale and break the complacency that had crept into the American efforts at the start of the war.

Patton transformed II Corps' culture immediately after assuming command. He replaced several ineffective commanders with leaders who shared his results-driven approach. He also rapidly improved morale by building confidence through delivering speeches, meeting his troops, and visiting the front lines regularly. Patton completely overhauled II Corps' operational tactics by emphasizing initiative.

NEVER OUTMATCHED

His approach focused on three main areas: discipline, coordination, and offense. He enforced tighter schedules and rigorous training, started enforcing uniform standards and helmet discipline, and focused on improving the coordination between the American land forces and the British air service that controlled the skies over the Mediterranean. Most famously, he shifted to aggressive strategies to take the fight to the Nazi forces.

---— ★ ---—

I don't want to hear about holding our position. We're not holding anything. Let the Hun do that. We are advancing constantly and we're not interested in holding on to anything except the enemy.
—Gen. George Patton, in the film *Patton*[6]

---— ★ ---—

After identifying numerous deficiencies in the American approach, Patton emphasized training his tank crews to combine more effectively with infantry, field artillery, and air support. The American tanks at the Kasserine Pass had been picked off in their unsupported frontal assaults by German anti-tank crews. He made technological improvements to bring in bigger guns for the Shermans, which were being outmatched by the Panzer and Tiger tanks. He also started adding armor to the lightly shelled American machines.

Within ninety days, the Allies defeated the Germans in North Africa in numerous engagements, finally causing 275,000 Axis troops to surrender.

The Battle of Kasserine Pass remains a notable example of how early setbacks in warfare can lead to significant improvements and eventual success if you have the right leader. The concept of "being outnumbered" goes beyond just the raw estimates of troop strength. From a military perspective, you can be—and often are—outnumbered in several areas, such as equipment, ammunition, support of the indigenous population, air support, troop experience, communications, and command experience.

This "outnumbered" concept shows up in the corporate world too. You can be outnumbered in many ways, including budget, staff, experience, products, geographies, features, innovation, and leadership. But that's not an excuse for lazy leadership.

The Board Didn't Hire You to Maintain the Status Quo

No one hires a new CMO and expects inaction. Don't put a status quo plaque on your desk.

It's hard to remember back to a time when photos were developed on actual film. I think back to 1995, when digital photography was still in its infancy. Kodak, the once-dominant player in film and photography, struggled to transition into the digital age. The digital transformation was Kodak's Kasserine Pass. Although

still dominant in some areas, they were slipping. They were clearly outnumbered in terms of innovation and speed to market, and the board recognized this.

--- ★ ---

Success in war depends on the golden rules of war: speed, simplicity, and boldness.
—Gen. George Patton[7]

--- ★ ---

In 1995, Kodak brought on John Sculley, who they thought would be their General Patton. The former Apple CEO was hired to be an innovator and to lead the pivot to the digital photography market.

However, employees were accustomed to a business model that revolved around physical film and printing, which had been highly profitable for decades.

This legacy mindset created friction, and Sculley's push to focus on long-term digital growth rather than short-term printing profits was met with resistance.

He was ousted in less than two years, and by 2012, Kodak was bankrupt. Despite the mandate to change, Kodak struggled to make structural and strategic changes. Sculley could not overcome an entrenched bureaucracy and a culture reliant on the declining film processing business. This is viewed as one of the great business cases of culture eating strategy.

Transforming Culture Requires More Than Vision

How many short-lived CMOs suffer from the Kodak example?

The average tenure of a chief marketing officer (CMO) has historically been one of the shortest among C-suite executives. According to Spencer Stuart's 2022 study on C-suite tenure, CMOs averaged just over four years. Meanwhile, a CEO averages almost seven years in their position.[8]

Why is there such high turnover among CMOs?

Some of the factors cited in Spencer Stuart's study as contributing to the higher turnover trend included,
- pressure to deliver results quickly,
- responding to changing markets,
- rapidly evolving digital trends, and
- difficulty demonstrating a return on investment for marketing initiatives.

To successfully overcome these factors, a CMO must be able to consider the best options quickly and decisively with a completely engaged team. Have confidence that you will not be outmatched.

---   ★   ---

Make sure you number yourself among your forces.
—*Noah benShea* [9]

---   ★   ---

During my many years working in behavioral health, I've encountered interesting parallels between addressing business and marketing problems.

The challenge of distinguishing between contributing factors and determining factors may explain why we sometimes struggle to take decisive action.

In therapeutic relationships, therapists evaluate contributing factors and determining factors to correctly identify what is modifiable versus what is inherent to the client's condition. *Contributing* factors can be described as creating conditions that lead to vulnerability, while *determining* factors are elements that require direct intervention.

For example, a contributing factor to substance use disorder could be peer pressure or exposure to a social group that normalizes substance use. This exposure can increase your likelihood of using substances, but it does not guarantee it.

A determining factor related to substance use disorder is the physical dependence the body has developed to a substance and the subsequent compulsion to abuse it.

Mitigating contributing factors promotes resilience, but one has to address determining factors in order to alleviate the core symptoms and resolve immediate crises. Changing one's schedule or relocating can mitigate pressure from a social group (contributing factors) whereas seeking detox and getting inpatient treatment can solve the physical condition of a person's substance use disorder (determining factors).

In business, understanding the contributing factors will help clients see that their history and environment do not always define their present state, and understanding their determining factors can also encourage them to take actionable steps to improve.

As a leader, don't let contributing factors stop you from progressing toward your determining factors. You may have contributing factors like a tight budget that you will have to mitigate with creativity, staffing changes, or reallocation, but the environment of a budget constraint should not stop you from taking actionable steps within your budget.

Focusing on contributing factors will lead to a biased thought pattern. It becomes a cognitive distortion that negatively influences how you perceive yourself and the world around you, leading to heightened stress and anxiety that contributes to inaction.

Find a Quick Win

I like to use quick wins to gain momentum in my push to change a business's culture regarding its bigger systemic issues. Patton turned around II Corps in ninety days. He didn't waste a single day getting started.

Think about quick wins in the context of being outnumbered. You don't control your opponents' numbers, strategies, or plans. Quick wins get the ball moving and demonstrate that your approach will overcome your opponents' advantages.

★

It is in your moments of decision that your destiny is shaped.
—*Tony Robbins*[10]

★

What Stops Us from Taking Action?

For young leaders, underestimation can be a fact of life. You're new to your role or your company, and while you were hired or promoted for your potential, you are still a newbie. Until you act, your success cannot be measured.

Some of the best examples of young leaders taking action come from the battlefield.

In April 1429, Joan arrived at the French court of Charles VII and convinced the monarch to send her to Orléans with a relief force. During the Hundred

OUTNUMBERED BUT NEVER OUTMATCHED

Years' War, the British had laid siege to Orléans, the last major city defending the Loire Valley, and its fall could have opened all of France to English conquest. When Joan arrived in the beleaguered city, she encountered a demoralized defense with dwindling supplies. She convinced the defenders to adopt her strategic vision, rooted in going on the offensive. The French had relied on defending the city with only piecemeal skirmishes and prolonged negotiations with the British. Joan's strategy was to attack the English fortifications surrounding the city directly.

On May 4, just a few days after her arrival in Orléans, Joan led an assault on a key English position at the Saint-Loup bastion. Her forces captured it after fierce fighting, marking the first major French victory in the campaign. Two days later, she rallied her troops and fought on the front lines as the French captured the English stronghold of Saint-Jean-le-Blanc. She followed up that victory the next day at the decisive assault on the Tourelles gate, a heavily fortified English outpost on the Loire River. Joan, despite sustaining an arrow wound, encouraged her forces to press forward and personally led the charge. Her bravery inspired the French to overwhelm the English defenders and secure the fort. On May 8, 1429, the English abandoned their siege and retreated, marking a turning point in the war.

Joan's strategy of direct engagement and assaults on the British positions were in direct contrast to the status quo. Yet her singular belief in her mission rallied her monarch, soldiers, and countrymen to her strategy, and her presence on the battlefield further inspired her troops.

Sometimes, the leader has to be the first one in and the last one out to get the ball rolling.

---★---

**Courage! Ne reculez pas.
(Courage! Do not fall back.)**
—*Joan of Arc*[11]

---★---

Nothing Ever Goes to Plan

Epaminondas was a Theban general who, in the fourth century BCE, executed one of the most storied maneuvers in military history to decisively win a battle over the larger and more experienced Spartan army.

The standard military tactic among Greek city-states at the time was to place their best soldiers on the right side of the battle formation. Epaminondas broke that tradition and placed his elite forces in the center. He then cleverly pulled additional fighters from his flanks to make the depth of his forces fifty men deep versus the typical Spartan formation of eight to twelve men deep. Knowing the outside flanks of his formation were now weak, he echeloned those forces on the edge and instructed them to use delaying tactics to avoid becoming fully engaged and potentially overrun. His engaged center now had an overwhelming force that decisively neutralized the Spartans.

He knew he was outnumbered that day, but he did not let the contributing factor of his opponent's size deter him. Instead he exercised his creativity in crafting a battle plan—one that used all the soldiers and weapons he brought onto the battlefield in an ingenious way.

★

Some leaders stick their heads in the sand and claim they are in a sandstorm.
—Noah benShea[12]

★

So, what's the lesson for us?

Instead of complaining that your area is underfunded, you could spend your budget more creatively. Perhaps you pause a marketing channel like television or billboard to load up on paid search for a few weeks or months. Instead of hiring a hard-to-find senior person, maybe hire a less experienced but highly motivated junior. Perhaps a person on your team would be interested in a stretch assignment to cover a key unsupported area. Think about shifting your coverage of geographies in order to overwhelm one area with extra staff and attention.

★

The art of war is to gain more from favorable circumstances than they yield by their own nature.
—Napoleon Bonaparte[13]

★

At Foundations, our oldest facility, La Paloma (later renamed The Oaks at La Paloma), struggled with deferred maintenance issues over the years. The staff cared for our patients, but the grounds and facilities were always a challenge to maintain due to its almost hundred-year-old buildings and sprawling urban footprint (twelve acres) in a high-traffic part of Memphis. As we worked to reimagine the facility (more on that in a later chapter), our corporate staff knew we had an opportunity to help immediately while our marketing team prepared the plan and budget.

We aimed to maintain a patient census of 85 percent of our capacity. That goal had started to slip some months prior, so bold action was required on our team's part. While we were crafting the new marketing strategy to address the declining census, we decided to take immediate action while website changes, videos, print collateral, and earned media were all being planned and coordinated.

I knew that esprit de corps—a sense of pride among the group or team—would be critical in our plan. We needed to instill in our staff and alumni the sense of pride that had been lost over time. I was also aware that we needed strong cohesion with the facility staff so our plans and ideas would not be interpreted as taking over or telling them what to do. Our Memphis team needed to see the Nashville corporate staff as mutual support of our collective goals for the facility.

No battle plan survives contact with the enemy. Leadership is the art of accomplishing more than the science of management says is possible.
—Gen. Colin Powell[14]

We took a group of our marketing team over to Memphis to create an overwhelming force that would help the local staff fix some of the problems that had plagued the facility for years. Like Epaminondas, we had the soldiers that we had—that is, I had only my current staff and my current budget.

Like one of the home renovations shows you see on HGTV, we worked with the facility CEO, Dave Perez, to create a two-day rejuvenation event. We showed up en masse with rolled-up sleeves and a service-oriented attitude. We split into teams, tackling everything from trash and debris removal to paint touch-ups to reorganizing the gym. Our marketing team traffic manager, Melanie Melcher, pulled twenty-three tires from one side of the property bordering a busy road that had been used as an illegal dumping area for years. Our podcast producer, David Condos, drove the Bobcat and cleared large areas that had become overgrown.

This team of web developers, videographers, copywriters, social media analysts, data analysts, and graphic designers all repositioned themselves for two days to help us accomplish a vital marketing effort beyond what they normally do. We could have just done our digital work remotely, but we would not have had an impact on what was really important: restoring pride from the staff, alumni, and community for this historic institution that had successfully treated so many people.

OUTNUMBERED BUT NEVER OUTMATCHED

You have much more in you than you sometimes give yourself credit for. Rather than fixate on what you are missing, take a fresh look at what you have. Get creative. Move things around. Focus all your cannons on one target for a short period. Be present and lead the charge yourself. You may be outnumbered, but with the right plan, attitude, and commitment, you'll never be outmatched.

WHAT NEXT?

 Apply this with your team.
Look for ways to focus your team's efforts on one marketing area like a laser beam. Use that focus like Epaminondas to win in that area. Then, redeploy and continue.

 Apply this with your C-suite.
Make sure your key performance indicators are *your* key indicators. Educate your C-suite on new metrics that you use to drive the business. Run the old KPIs in parallel with the new KPIs to build trust.

 Earn a quick win.
Solve a marketing conundrum quickly with your limited resources by focusing everyone briefly on solving the problem. For example, you might have everyone pitch in on a new landing page, a conference, or a video shoot and rollout. Whatever it is, find one area in your business that could benefit from short-term intensity and focus, then send your troops into battle.

Chapter 2

COMMANDER'S INTENT

Decisions, decisions, decisions.

We make decisions daily—operational decisions like scheduling and tactical decisions like staffing and project deployment. We have programmed decisions like staff reviews and status reports. We participate in group decisions with budget committees and execute rational decisions like running the cost-benefit analysis of a new product. We make simple decisions like ordering office supplies. We are called on to make crisis decisions, such as dealing with a cybersecurity breach. But how do we encourage strategic decision-making? Strategic decision-making shouldn't just be left to the CEO. Strategic thinking is long-term and broad in scope—and this type of thinking should apply across the whole organization, not only the highest level of leadership.

NEVER OUTMATCHED

--- ★ ---

A good plan, violently executed now, is better than a perfect plan executed next week.
—Gen. George S. Patton[15]

--- ★ ---

A foundational principle in military operations is *commander's intent*. It encapsulates decentralized decision-making and empowers subordinates to take action within a shared framework of understanding, a strategic framework. This decision-making process is iterative, and commanders at each level must continuously assess the situation and adjust their decisions to accomplish the mission.

During medieval times, warfare was conducted by centralized command structures, often requiring strict adherence to specific orders primarily due to limited means of communication. Flags and banners were used as signals to relay the location of commanders and troop units. Banner colors, shapes, and directional movements of flags all signaled specific commands such as advance, retreat, or regroup. In addition, a medieval battlefield would be alive with the sound of drums and trumpets that conveyed orders to charge or signaled a warning. The noise and chaos of the battlefield often interfered with medieval armies' ability to communicate. In some instances, opposing forces captured flags

COMMANDER'S INTENT

and banners and sowed confusion by signaling false information.

The hierarchical approach to decision-making drove these primitive methods. All decisions had to come from the king, queen, emperor, or general.

Napoleon was an early innovator in encouraging decision-making as close to the front lines as possible and in real time. His *corps d'armée* system trained officers to understand the strategic intent and allowed them some operational independence in order to achieve it. His field marshals were empowered to take action as the battle evolved rather than waiting for specific instructions.

Carl von Clausewitz further influenced this approach. The Prussian military formalized a doctrine of mission-type orders known as *Auftragstaktik*. This doctrine emphasized that subordinates had a clear mission but also had the freedom to determine how they would achieve it.

---- ★ ----

No plan survives first contact with the enemy.
—*Helmuth von Moltke*[16]

---- ★ ----

In many of my coaching sessions with young leaders, I will ask them, "In your role, are you a manager or a leader?"

Our lower-echelon leaders often have the title of manager or director even if they aren't actually *managing* or *directing* much of anything. A manager will operate in a world of repetitive, operational, and simple decisions, and they can become very efficient in that process. At times, there is a disconnect between the human resources job description or job code that was selected in the payroll system and what the CEO, CMO, or board wants a manager to do, which is deliver commander's intent.

Is it their role to manage, approve timecards, process expense reports, create monthly reports, conduct annual reviews, manage paid time off, interview candidates, or order equipment? The answer is yes. But while that is a part of their job, it should be a minor part of it.

The board and the CEO have set their commander's intent. The leader's role is to receive that commander's intent and pass it on to their team. That's where leading is critical, and it's at the heart of what a CEO and board need for their managers and directors to be successful.

★

You manage things; you lead people.
—*Rear Adm. Grace Hopper*[17]

★

Why do some people retreat into the manager role rather than seize the responsibility to lead? You have to look up the chain of command. Do the leaders above them demonstrate the commander's intent, or have they inadvertently created a hierarchical system?

The United States military formally adopted aspects of *Auftragstaktik* into its doctrine during the Cold War. It recognized the value of empowering lower-echelon commanders, the captains, and lieutenants who were doing the fighting and closest to the action. The US Army's Field Manual 100-5 (*Operations*), published in 1982, highlighted the concept of commander's intent as a critical element in mission command. It emphasized understanding the desired end state and enabling initiative.

Commander's intent is defined as "a clear and concise expression of the purpose of the operation and the desired military end state."[18]

Does your team know the "desired end state" and that exercising initiative can help them achieve it? The word *initiative* is so important, especially in a marketing sense. We want our staff to take initiative, so why is it so hard for them to execute it to achieve the desired end state? Do your leaders give the commander's intent, or do they micromanage? Do your leaders even know you have given them your commander's intent?

In a military sense, failure to understand the desired end state and use initiative can have devastating results. The French loss against the English in 1346 at the Battle of Crécy is an excellent example. The French, confident in their military superiority, sent waves of knights up a muddy embankment in charges.

The French king, Philip VI, was present on the battlefield but could not effectively impose order (communicate the desired end state) and adjust to the changing circumstances (take initiative). Instead of adapting, the French commanders persisted stubbornly in their rigid and predictable approach. The commanders closest to the battle failed to exercise initiative since this was not in their command structure's DNA. They could have halted the reckless charges and adapted by attempting flanking maneuvers. The French command's lack of proactive decision-making at lower levels doomed them.[19]

A similar lack of decision-making throughout an organization can be seen in Elizabeth Holmes's company, Theranos. Holmes envisioned revolutionizing health care with a device that could run multiple diagnostic tests from a single drop of blood. While ambitious, this vision relied on unproven technology. Her new testing device failed to meet the early vision and achieve the promised results. Instead of adapting the business model or refining the product, Holmes continued to push forward with exaggerated claims. There were many issues in the company's ultimate failure regarding ethics and a refusal to adapt strategies, but corporate secrecy and the lack of commander's intent stand out to me.

COMMANDER'S INTENT

Instead of fostering an adaptive and open company culture, Holmes operated in secrecy, preventing the company from acknowledging and addressing problems that could have been resolved. Instead of sharing her commander's intent, Holmes shut her lower-echelon commanders out of the decision-making process. Even their company-wide meetings were heavily scripted and controlled. Many employees reported that the culture at Theranos discouraged transparency and open communication, and information was heavily siloed.[20]

Like the French losses seven hundred years earlier, Holmes's once-promising idea failed. Leaders must be willing to pivot when faced with challenges or evidence that their initial approach isn't working. The commander's intent is critical to fostering that innovative culture.

In the 1970s, 3M was known for its innovative culture that created diverse product lines. Products like ScotchGuard, sandpaper, magnetic audio tapes, and reflective products for signs and clothing all started at 3M. Spencer Silver, one of 3M's chemical engineers, created a unique, low-tack adhesive that could stick to surfaces but be easily removed without leaving residue. At first, no one at 3M could figure out a practical application.

Art Fry, another chemical engineer at 3M, was an avid singer in his church choir. He found it frustrating when bookmarks slipped out of his hymnbook. One day, he realized that Silver's low-tack adhesive could

be perfect for a type of bookmark for his hymnal. He decided to experiment with the adhesive on small pieces of paper. He championed the idea, overcoming skepticism from colleagues and managers who doubted the market potential.

Post-it notes officially launched in 1980 and became a massive success. Now one of 3M's iconic products, they're sold worldwide and generate billions of dollars in revenue.[21]

Are You Communicating Your Commander's Intent?

Do you and your company give commander's intent to leaders down the line? Do your leaders know the mission and have the freedom to move? The next time someone on your staff brainstorms about social media, reels, or TikTok, do they understand your commander's intent and your support in investigating whether those tools enhance the completion of the mission? When staffers want to explore new geographies or territories, do they have room to do so? Can team members act when they have ideas for new conferences or webinars? When a designer wants to test new calls to action on your website or implement live chat or forms, can they set up a test independently?

Giving commander's intent is not permission to act foolishly or to waste time, money, or resources. It's executed within your company's governance and organizational framework and budget. Don't let fear or control stop you and your team from executing your mission.

Some Leaders Are "Built Different"

For some team leaders, commander's intent is innate in their approach to life. They ask for forgiveness rather than permission from team members.

A leader not very well known in the West is Rani Lakshmibai, the queen of Jhansi. She is well known in India for leading her kingdom's resistance against British colonial forces during the First War of Indian Independence (1857–58). She was not born or appointed to lead a rebellion. Her husband, Maharaja Gangadhar Rao, passed away in 1853, and the British East India Company refused to recognize their adopted son as the rightful heir. At that time, the British applied the doctrine of lapse, which allowed them to annex any princely state without a direct male heir. The Jhansi territory was annexed, and Queen Rani Lakshmibai was ordered by force to leave the fort.

Queen Rani heeded something innate in her DNA and organized the village militias. Traditionally, the Kshatriya caste (warriors) was associated with military roles, while other castes were excluded from such duties. She decided to innovate, mobilize, and train an army that would include men and women from different castes and communities, breaking the traditional norms to strengthen her forces.

The caste system was deeply entrenched in Indian society at the time. Her army included Dalits, Brahmins, Kshatriyas, Vaishyas, and Shudras, who fought side by side, breaking traditional norms of segregation. The Brahmins represented priests, teachers, and scholars. The Dalits, known as the "untouchables," performed tasks considered impure or polluting, such as cleaning, leatherwork, and cremation. For Rani to unite all groups, from the marginalized to the highest caste, was earth-shattering in Indian culture.

Rani continued her break with tradition by altering familiar gender roles of Indian society. Women, especially from upper castes, were expected to adhere to domestic roles. Her active leadership on the battlefield was a direct challenge to these norms. Her courage and inspiration became a symbol for people from all backgrounds to break from the rigid roles assigned by caste and gender.

She used her prerogative. In a time when societal hierarchies and rigid caste distinctions were deeply entrenched, her strategy was revolutionary and instrumental in uniting her forces against the British. She was clear in her mission to uphold her kingdom's sovereignty and resist annexation. She would not be deterred by the traditional norms that would have cut her forces dramatically. Her commanders knew the bigger picture and had the freedom to exercise nontraditional and innovative ideas to accomplish the mission.

Queen Rani didn't wait or seek permission; she took action as a commander. She exercised her commander's intent, and her captains and lieutenants built an army that would not have been possible if they had adhered to the traditional models of the time. Her inclusive approach to building her army became the model for the independence movement later led by Mahatma Gandhi. Queen Rani's team understood the desired end state and enabled initiative.[22]

★

What is required of an officer is a certain power of discrimination, which only knowledge of men and things and good judgement can give.
—*Carl von Clausewitz*[23]

★

You Can't Command Innovation

Do the leaders on your team have the support they need to challenge conventional thinking in your marketing and your business?

You cannot command, direct, or order innovation. However, you can communicate your commander's intent on the goal and then ensure that you have enabled your team to exercise creativity and initiative within your company's structure and governance.

Inaction kills teams and a company's success. Bureaucracy can create an environment in which leaders and team members are afraid to act, creating the dreaded "It's not in my budget" or "It's not in my job description" mentality.

COMMANDER'S INTENT

I was working with a consulting client in North Carolina recently, and as part of my analysis, I interviewed as many people as possible related to marketing and operations. As I was talking with one of the marketing channel team leads, I casually asked why her team had stopped using an app designed to communicate with former patients. She didn't know. I asked if it was a budgetary decision. She replied she wasn't sure and didn't have access to the budget. As I interviewed the CEO, he felt he had delivered the mission and his commander's intent to grow that marketing channel, but the empowerment was obviously missing from his junior leader. Sometimes, we as leaders feel confident in our actions, but we can easily overlook whether the commanders below us feel empowered.

In many military situations, soldiers use the *readback*, the practice of reading back the order or message to ensure it is understood correctly. The readback provides an opportunity to catch any discrepancies and confirm the communication. The readback strategy could provide an opening for further conversation with younger leaders who are new to exercising the commander's intent.

The Buck Stops Where?

I have been fortunate to work for big companies, medium-size companies, and start-ups. At Perot Systems, I came into an organization that was very mature in processes and procedures. The onboarding process included detailed checklists for employees and leaders, all designed to make sure new hires hit the ground running. But that wasn't all. We also heard regularly from Ross Perot Sr. about what his commander's intent was, and it flowed down through the leadership chain.

In contrast, when I worked for a start-up, everything was so hectic and everyone was wearing so many hats that I was thrilled they had successfully collected my direct deposit information for payroll. Yet even in those chaotic times, the founders never failed to communicate their commander's intent to sell digital music.

Commander's intent is adopted to ensure that your staff knows the end goal, the mission. It ensures that subordinates know they are encouraged to achieve their goals creatively. They know not to wait. Most small and medium-size companies do not have the documented processes and procedures that can sometimes mask a commander's intent. Checklists, procedures, and documentation will help you get your job done, but it's not commander's intent. Your leaders need to hear that your organization succeeds if they acknowledge the mission and then make decisions to execute it.

Who is at fault when a leader oversees a team of individuals or an important process and does not know the budget? If there is commander's intent, those leaders will dig into that budget because they are preparing to take action. If a leader waits around for months because they don't know their budget, it is not just that person's problem; it's the commander's problem farther up the chain of command. The whole organization has to have commander's intent.

I've encountered situations on numerous occasions in which CMOs and marketing directors were hired but then told that certain people they managed were untouchable, meaning those individuals could not be let go. Similarly, I've experienced leaders being stuck with certain vendors or platforms. The company has hired this new leader and given them the mission but has hamstringed their ability to act and impeded their freedom of movement to accomplish the mission. It's a recipe for disaster.

★

Pursue your opportunities vigorously. Recognize that you will have less capital and fewer people than your mature competitors. Use brains, wits and creativity as substitutes for money and you will have a clear advantage over your wealthy competitors.
—Ross Perot[24]

★

The Checklist Mentality

When I arrive at a company to start a consulting analysis, I often receive lots of pretty reports. As I sit with the leader to learn about these reports, I am always astounded by how proud they can be with a large volume of paper. Usually, if they've had to bring me in, things are not going as expected, and the CEO or board is looking for answers, a solution, and a path forward. I review the stack of paper and see that the reports themselves have become the goal for certain leaders—simply producing the reports and sending them up the chain of command. Pages of keywords and phrases, bounce rates, percentages of traffic sources, device percentages, top landing pages, and hundreds of other data points are produced in beautiful pie charts and line graphs.

It's what I refer to as the *checklist mentality*: The boss wants reports, so I'll check that off my task list for this month. In a military situation, the checklist mentality doesn't work. Just checking things off will get your position overrun or worse.

Instead, the army adopts the concept of a SITREP, or situation report. It includes a date and time, a summary situation overview, the actions completed, the next steps, any critical incidents, and any requests for support. The idea is to keep the chain of command informed but minimize the bureaucracy. The SITREP keeps the focus on commander's intent.

Information is critical to your success, but don't get lost in the goal of collecting and sharing it. Instead, use it for making decisions. A SITREP for your team is going to be personal. You will create it the same way you establish your KPIs.

COMMANDER'S INTENT

Early on at Foundations, there was a routine around understanding the number of admissions for each day. That daily figure gave me very little information on our pipeline and how our marketing channels looked in the days to come for admissions. Admissions were old data for me. Admission to a program cannot happen without a lead, a lead cannot happen without a phone call, and a phone call cannot happen without a marketing activity like a website visit. It was done manually at first, and we later automated and displayed our SITREP in real time.

How Do You Know If Your Team Has Commander's Intent?

To know whether your team understands the commander's intent, you first have to be present for your direct reports. Can you imagine being in battle without talking with your direct reports for a few days, let alone a few weeks? There has to be regular communication. This is the first part of understanding the commander's intent. Are you regularly giving and reinforcing the concept?

Adopt the concept of a readback. This communication practice is used to ensure that commands and critical information are accurately received and understood. It involves the recipient repeating the information to the issuer verbatim or in a summarized form. This process is crucial in high-stakes environments where miscommunication can lead to serious consequences. It ensures both parties have the same understanding and can correct any misunderstanding. This can also help your team standardize their communication and help focus the message on comprehension.

Second, recognize and reward behavior that applies commander's intent. You've encouraged creativity and reinforced your team's freedom of movement; now recognize the behavior you want them to keep replicating. Take time in your staff meetings to call out instances when commander's intent has been followed—it's not just a matter of telling them; you now have examples of the team applying it.

Third, add commander's intent to your team's key performance indicators (KPIs). Don't assume what your predecessor used is the best system or that it covers everything you need. Use your prerogative to add or to better define measurements if required.

One of my clients was reporting leads monthly. I was trying to help them figure out why conversions seemed so low. They had a high volume of leads but a troublingly low conversion rate. As I looked at the details, I saw many of the leads were nothing more than a first name and last name. That was a great find because when they reviewed the data the leaders realized they had been making assumptions that the leads were of higher quality. We quickly got on a whiteboard, defined what constitutes a lead, and then programmatically updated the CRM so it would not save the lead without the mandatory fields. Going forward, it did two things for us: It ensured we had defined leads with more data and contact points for follow-up, and it required the agents on the phone to spend more time with the callers in order to get the information, which opened up more opportunities for them to convert.

Throughout your business career, there are going to be times when you need things like experience, certificates, or bigger budgets to contribute to your success. Those can often be hard to find, but commander's intent is free, and you can use it today to help you win.

WHAT NEXT?

 Apply this with your team.
Apply the readback method. Ask team members to repeat your desired end state and your commander's intent. Have them do a readback with their teams. Share as a group any opportunities for miscommunications that were caught during the readback.

 Apply this with your C-suite.
Share how leaders on your team are exercising commander's intent. Use that language and mention how your subordinates took the initiative as a result.

 Gain a quick win.
Put together your SITREP and share.

Chapter 3

CITIZEN FARMER, CITIZEN SOLDIER

Historically, few societies had professional armies 365 days a year. Most cultures maintained a strong connection between farming and fighting.

You can trace part-time soldiers back thousands of years to the Greek hoplites (their citizen soldiers) in the phalanx and the Roman land-owning farmers joining the famed legions. These systems held the belief that their civic duty was also tied to their vested interest in defending the republic. Their evolution directly relates to our modern-day structure of squads, companies, battalions, and regiments.

During the American Revolutionary War, many colonists were farmers by trade but also served as militia members known as Minutemen. These colonialist farmers-turned-soldiers played a crucial role in the early battles of the Revolution, including the pivotal Battles of Lexington and Concord in 1775. They were ready to fight on short notice, hence the name "Minutemen."

In more modern times, we overlook Switzerland when discussing military tactics, but they have a long tradition of military excellence. It starts with their idea of a citizen army, with many of its soldiers historically coming from rural areas and working as farmers. The Swiss military system relies on a militia of trained citizen soldiers to defend the country. In peacetime, many return to farming and other civilian occupations.

There were also the Boers, the Dutch settlers in South Africa who were predominantly farmers and formed a militia system known as commandos during the Boer Wars against the British. These farmer-soldiers used their knowledge of the land and guerrilla tactics to resist British forces, demonstrating farmers' dual role as civilians and soldiers.

Ancient armies did have some smaller groups of professional soldiers in their ranks, but most Greek and Roman soldiers were farmers first in their societies. Why didn't they turn every soldier into a professional instead of allowing them to return home to their professions after times of upheaval?

It's because they could be relied on without question. It wasn't as if a bunch of medieval peasants were sitting around untrained or that the farmers were the only people around for the king to grab. No, these farmers' approaches to farming correlated to their success in the military. Operations and approaches to agriculture and the military synced up. The agricultural and military models were aligned.

They were disciplined and organized. They were citizen farmers, citizen soldiers.

--- ★ ---

The cultivators of the earth are the most valuable citizens. They are the most vigorous, the most independent, the most virtuous, and they are tied to their country and wedded to its liberty and interests by the most lasting bonds.
—Thomas Jefferson[25]

--- ★ ---

All Hands on Deck

Your entire staff has to be ready to jump in when called and be part of marketing. When we go to conferences, we always like to have a clinical person come with us, whether at the booth or giving a talk. We tell them, "Put on your marketing hat."

In early Roman times, military service was directly linked to land ownership. For citizens who owned land, serving in the military was part of their civic duty. Farmers made up a large slice of Roman society, and this temporary service allowed Rome to quickly stand up a well-trained and qualified army in times of conflict. Being both a citizen and a soldier was a key aspect of

Roman identity. This dual role of farmer and soldier embodied classical Roman values such as discipline, loyalty, and service.

Similarly, staff, referral sources, and alumni all have their day jobs—their citizen farmer roles. To force-multiply your marketing beyond your marketing team, you must empower them to see their roles as citizen soldiers. After all, who is closer to our consumers, clients, and patients than our employees and staff? Surely, inspiring them to engage in our marketing efforts in a meaningful way could lead to one of our most enduring successes in marketing.

Being called on in time of need is not a civic duty but a corporate one. The word *corporate* originates from the Latin word *corporatus*, meaning "formed into a body." Corporate duty for your citizen soldiers means defending your collective organization. It's helping your teams and supporting their shared values and beliefs.

In my role as chief marketing officer at Foundations Recovery Network, one of our main marketing channels was through our alumni. However, we didn't classify our alumni channel as former patients. Former patients who were *returning* to us were tracked as readmissions. But a former patient (or their family) who was *referring* someone to us fell in the alumni bucket. We wanted our alumni to be engaged and to multiply our marketing efforts. We viewed alumni and their immediate family members as part of our citizen soldier army.

Igniting the family's participation multiplied the effect of our outreach through alumni. I could talk to one alumnus, but bringing the family along in those marketing journeys wasn't much more effort.

In fact, our approach to sparking our alumni and their families had four phases:

1. Ignite
2. Action
3. Learning
4. Return the Favor

The first three phases were about motivating them to participate, stay engaged, and continue to learn about their recovery. It wasn't until the final phase that we were specifically educating them on how to be active in sharing their success and referring others to seek the same treatment.

As we reviewed how to energize and grow our efforts through our alumni, we realized our call to action was thin. This was around the summer of 2011, and former First Lady Betty Ford had just passed away. During one of our weekly team meetings, we reflected on Betty Ford's impact on our industry and people in recovery as a group.

Betty Ford's activism began in 1974, when she shared her diagnosis of breast cancer. The press didn't even call it breast cancer back then; it was referred to in the media as "female cancer." Sharing her struggle while her husband was the sitting president of the United States was momentous. Following her lead, women in America started getting checked and openly discussing the rates of breast cancer with their families and doctors. The incidence of breast cancer spiked in the years immediately after the publicity around her case. This spike, known as the Betty Ford Blip, was not because of an increased incidence of breast cancer but because more women were seeking care. From the 1980s onward, rates of breast cancer death started declining due to early detection, reduced smoking, and new care options.[26]

---★---

Being ladylike does not require silence.
—*Betty Ford*[27]

---★---

Two years after her cancer news, Betty Ford shared her struggle with alcoholism.

Our team sat together and reflected on the contrast between what had happened in the country around those two issues—breast cancer and alcoholism—in the years since Betty Ford's very public health battles. Breast cancer awareness had come a long way in "polite" American society. Thanks to Betty Ford and later the Susan G. Komen Foundation, money and attention were regularly given to breast cancer –related charities. Most communities had awareness days, and even the NFL players wore pink to highlight the cause. Annually, the Susan G. Komen Race for the Cure 5K hosts 1.7 million participants.[28]

However, we had to admit that the disease of alcohol and drug addiction was still stigmatized. We needed a Betty Ford Blip for addiction awareness to remove the stigma around the concept of addiction as a disease. It was easier to talk about illnesses of the body versus illnesses of the brain. I once interviewed former US Congressman Patrick Kennedy, who agreed with our approach. "Take away the mysterious quality of mental health treatment," he said, "and get back to how we treat other chronic illnesses of other organs in the body."

Heroes in Recovery

I contacted Geno Church, speaker and Word of Mouth Marketing Hall of Famer, in Greenville, South Carolina. I saw Geno speak at a digital marketing conference in Nashville earlier that year. He presented a case study on a group called Love146.

Geno and his cofounders at the marketing agency Brains on Fire had rebranded and helped relaunch Love146. Its founder, Rob Morris, told the Brains on Fire team about the work they were doing to combat child sex trafficking. At the time, their foundation was called the International Child Justice Foundation.

Morris shared how the work they were doing and their name would at times overwhelm people, making it difficult to fundraise and hire.

When you have that kind of challenge, how can you ignite your citizen farmers? Through their work over many weeks, Morris told Geno's team a story of working on a secret mission in Asia to rescue kids actually being sold in a market. He described the scene perfectly, right down to the look of desperation in one child's eyes. The girl was staring at Morris from behind the bars of her little cell—cell 146. That was the hook Geno knew they needed to make an immediate impact. Hence the name, Love146.

Geno's presentation at that digital marketing conference was so powerful that I knew I'd love to engage him and his agency someday. That day had come. I arranged for some of my leaders to fly out with me to Greenville and meet Geno and Robin Phillips, his cofounder at Brains on Fire.

I explained to them our desire to create a social movement to foster the recovery blip. I desperately wanted to remove the stigma. After numerous conversations, we eventually secured a six-figure proposal for Brains on Fire to help us conceptualize and execute the vision.

Now, the tough part was getting agreement on the spending internally.

Force multiplication was the answer.

As I built the budget, I could see multiple areas benefiting from the initiative: digital marketing, professional referrals, alumni, internal communications, employee retention, and a really big issue in health care, staff recruiting. I ran the calculations. This movement was going to propel our engagement of our citizen farmers.

We envisioned collecting one thousand stories from people who were successful in their recovery. Those stories would become the backbone of a new website now seeded with more than a thousand pages of content. The story mechanism would be wrapped into our alumni program, giving alumni another activation point. At that point, alumni referrals were our third-largest referral channel. This could eventually account for a substantial portion of our social media engagement, and conservatively we could expect multiple videos per month for our YouTube page.

I also imagined that we would tie this into our two (at the time) national conferences. The icing on the cake was that we created a series of running events to get the message into the community. We launched those races in local areas where we had inpatient or outpatient facilities, creating a news story, employee engagement, and events that our referral sources, our alumni, and their families could attend.

The $150,000 investment suddenly became a story of thousands of touchpoints, exponentially growing our reach and content. Each area carried some of the cost and derived much more revenue from associated admissions. In addition, now when our recruiters were talking about our company, we had a differentiator. Who wouldn't want to work for a company that was so engaged? It built on our core mission and gave it an activation point, an outlet to go out into the community as citizen-famers-turned-citizen-soldiers.

Brains on Fire delivered the Heroes in Recovery concept. The deck I presented had all the wonderful graphic design concepts, the storyboards imagining Heroes being presented at conferences, our alumni gatherings, and our clinical staff.

The most important part was the math slides—the calculations on how the investment would deliver a return. I was able to document the search engine optimization gains, the improved conversion scores, the growth in alumni engagement and referrals, and the increase in geographical coverage for our marketing. Those were the slides the decision rested on.

We launched in early 2012 and soon surpassed our planned one thousand stories. Heroes quickly became ingrained in our alumni program, which increased membership and referrals. HR and recruiting used the concept to align our corporate values and ease the strain on filling positions. Our Heroes in Recovery 6K Run/Walk series eventually grew to a dozen events each year around the country. At our national conferences, we delivered annual Heroes in Recovery awards to honor clinicians and gave out youth scholarships through our Heroes essay contest.

With our social movement Heroes in place, our staff now had the story to describe why they do what they do. There are more than seventeen thousand substance abuse treatment centers in the United States. How do you decide where you want to work? The passion and dedication on display at Heroes events gave our staffing and recruiting team a distinct advantage. You don't jump into behavioral health care for the money; there is always an element of service. Heroes in Recovery gives voice to why our employees choose to work with us and volunteer on their days off. Besides handing the client our name and phone number, the referent had an easy and succinct way of connecting our physical program and services to our heart, which was the *why* behind our programs.

In 2017, I had the chance to interview Steve Ford, Betty Ford's son, on our *Recovery Unscripted* podcast about the impact she had on behavioral health. He shared, "It turned the recovery community upside down and moved it forward."[29] I felt after speaking with him that we had also contributed to continuing the legacy of activism with our approach.

Retaining Citizens

I've often felt that one of the preeminent reasons to approach staff as citizen farmers and citizen soldiers lies in their citizenry: They are "citizens" of your company. If they are engaged in the business and are called on, they become more invested and ready to help you do battle. In return, you will see improved employee retention.

The direct costs of losing employees include fees to retain hiring agencies or referral commissions, internal human resource costs, and advertising for replacement openings. Additionally, severance costs, legal resources, and new-hire training can be steep.

Indirect costs—including lost productivity, the brain drain (institutional knowledge loss), the potential impact of negative reviews on sites like Glassdoor.com, poor word-of-mouth reputation, and the negative impact on morale—can all have devastating impacts.

The cost to replace an employee can be 30 percent for entry-level positions, rising to 150–200 percent for mid-level and senior roles. You could be talking about many weeks once you factor in the time it takes to create an updated job description, run it through approvals, and get it into your human resources system. After that, time is required for reviewing applications and résumés, scheduling interviews, and making offers. Then, once you find your new person, it takes another two to three weeks for them to put in their notices at the job they're leaving. You are now looking at months of loss.

Wouldn't it be easier to improve your retention rate just a little?

CITIZEN FARMER, CITIZEN SOLDIER

Many companies have created programs such as brand ambassadors for employees to join. General Electric (GE) recognized its large employee base as key to sharing its company culture with potential employees. Their "We Create the Future" efforts featured employee role models in their campaigns. These actual stories featured unenhanced, real staff photos. The authenticity created an environment where viewers could see themselves in similar roles at GE. The dollars spent on the campaigns attracted new applicants and represented an investment in current staff.[30]

Starbucks is another company that has an innovative approach to activating its citizen soldiers. It created the concept of viewing its employees as partners and provides detailed guidelines about employees' engagement on social media.

---★---

We're called partners because this isn't just a job, it's our passion. So, go ahead and share it!
—Excerpt from Starbucks' guidelines

---★---

Starbucks founder Howard Schultz explains in his book *Onward*, "[Employees] are the true ambassadors of our brand, the real merchants of romance, and as such the primary catalysts for delighting customers. [Employees] elevate the experience for each customer—something you can hardly accomplish with a billboard or a 30-second spot."[31]

Why are companies afraid to engage their citizen farmers as soldiers in building their businesses?

As Jim Harter explains in a 2024 Gallup study titled "The New Challenge of Engaging Younger Workers,"

> The percentage of engaged Gen X employees (born between 1965 and 1979) has declined by four points, from 35% to 31%, while the percentage of actively disengaged Gen X employees has increased by one point, from 17% to 18%. This means that Gen X employees have seen their engagement ratio drop from 2.1 to 1.7—for every actively disengaged employee, there are now less than two engaged ones.[32]

Many are fearful and perceive the risks as greater than the potential advantages. Some marketing leaders I've engaged with worry about losing control of their messaging or brand voice. They also worry about legal exposure or negative publicity. I see this regularly in my consulting when I set up guidelines for responding to online reviews and creating speaker bureaus.

Some companies obsess over the fact that the guidelines won't be followed accurately and therefore want to review each comment or response to reviews, which dramatically slows responses to days and weeks and sends a message of distrust to the staff.

Civic organizations, schools, and news organizations frequently request behavioral health speakers to discuss addiction and mental health issues in their local communities. For some of my clients, the process of training and trusting staff to perform these duties is painful. It comes down to a lack of trust in their employees, which is entirely misplaced.

A marketing leader once told me they would have to review anything their staff shared on social media. I reframed the conversation for them. They have already allowed their staff to fly around the country, set up meetings, and independently represent their services in demonstrations, networks, and sponsor events. They're spending real money and talking to real people every single day. It's the same risks. Just as you have requirements on expense reporting and reporting on sponsorships, you need guidelines for social media engagement. If you do not, you're missing out on a real opportunity to force multiply with your citizen farmers.

In my many years in the army, with the Perot presidential campaigns, with Perot Systems, and with Foundations, I was always excited about and striving to achieve each organization's high goals. I was also surrounded by others who felt the same way. I'm sure you have people in your organization who are just as enthusiastic about and dedicated to the work they're doing too. My point here is that you are not alone. You are not the only one who is passionate about your company's goals! You are likely surrounded by citizen farmers who are just waiting to be recognized and empowered to "storm the castles" as citizen soldiers.

WHAT NEXT?

 Apply this with your team.
Lead by example. You should be engaged and participate in the social networks you use. Why would your frontline staff get involved if you're not?

 Apply this with your C-suite.
Create your version of employee guidelines. Keep it simple to start. Look at best practices from industry leaders like Starbucks. Don't bureaucratize or drown this opportunity in committee. Share how this force multiplies with marketing and human resources. Get leaders in your company to participate, even if it's just a little bit.

 Gain a quick win.
Celebrate the moments that your newly activated citizen farmers start sharing your marketing creations on behalf of your company. Include these shares, testimonials, stories, and events that showcase the power of your citizen famers in your employee newsletters or marketing emails to provide consistent positive reinforcement.

Chapter 4

FORCE MULTIPLICATION

In ancient times, the biggest advantage kings and chieftains had in battling their enemies was mass—their large number of warriors, ships, arrows, chariots, or horses. Mass was critical in determining the outcomes of a battle in ancient times and, subsequently, where societies focused their resources on preparing for offensive operations or defensive preparations.

Simply put, the largest army usually won.

Combat back then was composed of large groups of individuals fighting one-on-one. As one soldier fell wounded, exhausted, or killed, the next rank behind would fill in and battle the opposing soldier. This continued up to the last rank.

The Greeks, Romans, and Carthaginians organized mass in different ways, but the volume of soldiers was always the starting point. The ability to overwhelm an opponent with shock and awe through their physical dominance was important. Ancient battles saw high attrition rates, and mass allowed armies to absorb the large losses and continue to fight.

The Greeks focused the organization of their mass through the phalanx, the Romans through the legion, and the Gauls through the wedge.

From a military perspective, ancient times were simpler times. But, as systems and environments mature, there always comes a point where innovation beats mass.

Greece didn't build its mass as a unified empire like Rome. It was made up of independent city-states such as Athens, Corinth, Sparta, and Thebes. They would unite to fight against outside common enemies like Persia and Macedonia and then fall back to internal rivalries that exacerbated economic decline. Later, as Philip II of Macedonia rose in power, he improved on the Greek phalanx and innovated new weapons for the growing Macedonian army. Those improvements in battle strategies and equipment led to the Greek city-states' eventual subjugation to Philip II and eventually his son Alexander the Great.

The Carthaginian Empire in present-day Tunisia experienced significant growth and territorial expansion through its maritime trade dominance. The wealth and power the Carthaginians attained through their extensive trade routes were put to use by hiring

FORCE MULTIPLICATION

a network of mercenary soldiers from neighboring Numidia, Spain, and Gaul. These mercenary units were less reliable than citizen soldiers, and the moment they were not paid or payment was delayed, unrest and rebellion swelled among the ranks. Carthage used its wealth through trade to buy military mass. It worked for a time until Rome's strong citizen military and political structure eventually allowed it to dominate the Mediterranean.[33]

As the Roman Empire expanded, maintaining its vast military and supporting infrastructure became increasingly unsustainable. The number of soldiers required to garrison all distant provinces and defend against external threats to those territories led the empire to use noncitizen mercenaries who were less loyal and more expensive. This recruitment challenge and the financial strain of shifting to a defensive posture by building walls and fortifications led to inflation and dissatisfaction among the populace. The Romans were now sliding into the trap the Carthaginians found themselves in. Maintaining their mass was a significant financial strain, and their citizen manpower was stretched to the breaking point. The continued downward cycle led to dissatisfaction among the population, which led to more political instability and further shrinking of the land they controlled. This culminated in the eventual collapse as barbarian tribes marauded through Roman territory.

Innovation Eventually Defeats Mass

The eventual downfall of mass is as true in business as it is in the military. Innovation eventually wins.

Blockbuster was founded in 1985 in Dallas, Texas, by a software entrepreneur in the oil and gas industry named David Cook. The video rental market was a dispersed retail landscape featuring mom-and-pop stores with different operating hours, different rental policies, and very few available movie titles. The stores were not necessarily family friendly or well maintained and clean.

Blockbuster entered the market with large, well-organized, well-lit, standardized stores. They had dozens of copies of popular movies. They partnered with studios to ensure they had the latest releases before the smaller video chains or independent stores. This partnership further solidified Blockbuster as the best place to rent movies. Their innovative use of data in their supply chain allowed them to optimize their inventory by region to match local demand for movie titles. If a movie was more popular in the south, they could move additional inventory from the west to meet the southern demand, for example. These early innovations beat out their rivals.

Blockbuster continued growing by opening new stores and acquiring smaller video rental chains to become the largest video business in the United States. In 1989, the company went public and expanded internationally. Blockbuster became a cultural icon, appearing on numerous television shows and movies.

At its peak in 2004, Blockbuster had approximately 9,094 stores worldwide. In 2000, just as Blockbuster was peaking, they had a chance to acquire Netflix for $50 million. They declined, banking instead on their mass position in the marketplace.[34]

Bad move.

As it always does, the landscape changed, led by competitors that innovated the way consumers watched movies. McDonald's set up a subsidiary, Redbox, to offer conveniently positioned movie rentals in forty thousand locations across the US at an aggressive price point of one-dollar-a-day rentals.[35]

Netflix emerged as a DVD rental-by-mail service, taking advantage of consumers' preference not to travel to stores. They then transitioned completely into streaming, cementing their leadership in the space as home high-speed Internet access accelerated.

By the mid-2000s, Blockbuster was struggling with declining revenue, mounting debt, and the changing landscape of digital media. Their dominant position in mass was now a weight around their neck rather than an advantage.

The company attempted to launch its own DVD-by-mail and streaming services but was unable to compete effectively. Their mass—embodied by their nine thousand physical locations—became a financial albatross and a liability as consumer preferences moved to convenience, mail order, and lower-cost streaming. The up-front capital required to lease and purchase physical VHS tapes and DVDs and reliance on late fees created a perfect storm. Netflix leapfrogged them in the mail and streaming services, and by 2010, Blockbuster entered bankruptcy.[36]

Blockbuster's legacy is a reminder of how quickly industries can change in the face of technological innovation. And this is not an isolated example. Avon, Kodak, and Hoover have very similar stories to tell.

---— ★ ---—

I firmly believe that if our online strategy had not been essentially abandoned, we'd be rivalling Netflix for the leadership position in the internet downloading business.
—*John Antioco, former Blockbuster CEO*[37]

---— ★ ---—

FORCE MULTIPLICATION

Digital Mass

The advantage of mass was also present in the early days of search engine optimization (SEO), where again, quantity (mass) beat out quality. Those first SEO practices focused heavily on techniques that could boost a website's search engine ranking, even if those techniques didn't necessarily improve the user experience.

Strategies like *keyword stuffing* were popular (because they worked). Companies would cram as many keywords into their content and their meta tags as possible. Others would create a network of linked websites, and the sheer volume of links would boost their rankings. Still others were creating low-quality content, generated in bulk and produced by hiring cheaper offshore writers.

Make no mistake, this was innovative marketing compared to the traditional print media that came before. But like mass in warfare, the environment evolves and matures. Search engine algorithms changed, and the popular keyword strategies were no longer effective.

In 2011, Google rolled out the Panda update to their algorithm. This update penalized sites with poor quality, sometimes plagiarized content. Almost every year since, Google has rolled out major updates:

- 2012: Penguin arrived, which targeted spammy backlinks favored by link-building farms.

- 2013: Hummingbird debuted to improve search queries focused on natural language and understanding context.
- 2014: The Pigeon update looked at local listings in a more important way and dramatically impacted businesses that focused on national accounts and had little local presence.
- 2015: Mobilegeddon rewarded websites with excellent mobile-first design experiences along with superior site-speed-related hosting and the weight of the website's code.[38]

The updates continued with RankBrain, Medic, BERT, Core Web Vitals, and Helpful Content Updates.

As was the case with Blockbuster, the businesses built on mass discovered not only that volume was no longer effective but that it became a driving force behind their failure. The spammy links, plagiarized content, and disregard for user experience (UX) no longer worked and negatively impacted their SEO.

The businesses hanging on to the older strategies failed like the armies that never evolved from a strategy focused on mass.

Innovation over Mass

What happens when you look to innovation instead of mass?

FORCE MULTIPLICATION

Foundations Recovery Network took a chance on me in 2008. I was not a traditional CIO (chief information officer). I was younger than most when I interviewed, my degree was in political science, and I had trained and come through the IT project management route.

The private equity firms backing Foundations were used to interviewing the forty-year IBM employee. In contrast, I'd most recently worked at a digital music start-up. Luckily for me, the founder was keen on a new approach to digital marketing.

When I started, I removed barriers. Literally. We knocked down the offices and moved out the cubes. A colleague and I rented a van, drove to the closest IKEA in Atlanta, and came back with adjustable desks, lamps, and plants. The current small team spent a day putting everything together. Initially, the team was one web developer, an IT help desk person, and an electronic medical records administrator.

Although I laid out the vision for using digital marketing to reach potential patients, I had inherited a conservative budget. The private equity sponsors and founder were interested in the future but still tied to traditional media. Believe it or not, we were spending over $1 million per year on Yellow Pages, which was a significant chunk of our marketing budget.

The Yellow Pages was once an innovative marketing approach. In the 1970s, the Yellow Pages rep entered the local pizza place and gave them a trial phone for free, exclusively taking calls from Yellow Pages customers. The phone started ringing off the hook with pizza orders. The rep returned next week and asked the store, "Want to keep the phone?" They did, and they paid for the privilege.

But those times were long gone by the time I started with Foundations. The readership of the Yellow Pages was declining, and when I began the role, we started tracking the source of phone calls and could see that call volume coming from the Yellow Pages was much lower than we were led to believe. We had more calls from Google than from the Yellow Pages.

But Foundations still had senior executives, much older than me, who thought the Yellow Pages was going to be around forever. Regardless of the data I shared, they weren't ready to accept that the Yellow Pages no longer worked and were not going to change simply because I said so. They were suspicious of spending money on digital. It didn't fit with their existing worldview.

That's when I introduced them to Carl von Clausewitz.

Clausewitz was a Prussian professional combat soldier and staff officer involved in numerous military campaigns. I studied his work while training at Fort Knox during my Armor Officer Basic Course, and his countless military theories can be seen across a number of historical battles.

FORCE MULTIPLICATION

Famous primarily as a military theorist interested in the examination of war, Clausewitz utilized the campaigns of Frederick the Great and Napoleon as frames of reference for his work. His thesis: A small advantage in leadership (experience and innovation) and firepower (weapons) can deliver a huge advantage to an army. This was an example of a *force multiplier*.

Napoleon's ability to rapidly maneuver his forces to the *Schwerpunkt*, the focal point, was crucial to his victory at the Battle of Austerlitz in 1805. Napoleon was facing a larger coalition army when he feigned weakness on his right flank. As the coalition forces focused their attack on the right, he hit the lightly defended center, splitting their armies and allowing the French forces to encircle and rout the retreating British, Russian, and Austrian troops.[39]

Another example of Clausewitzian force multiplication in action is from Frederick the Great's Battle of Leuthen during the Seven Years' War in late 1757. The Battle of Leuthen perfectly illustrates how a smaller, well-led force can defeat a larger one through the clever use of force multipliers.

The Austrian forces outnumbered Frederick's army. He used speed to strike the Austrian left flank suddenly, hitting them at their critical weak point, the enemy's center of gravity. He also used deception to mask his troop's oblique order of attack, leading the Austrians to believe he was retreating. Plus, he multiplied his forces by concentrating them on the left flank. The psychological impact on the Austrian troops further weakened their resolve.[40]

Clausewitzian theories are a great contrast to the mass tactics of ancient times. Clausewitz looked for employing numerous factors at once to create a factored advantage, the antithesis of mass that uses only a single or small number of potential factors. Clausewitz had a formula for his thesis:

$$X^2 - Y^2 = \text{The Advantage}$$

An example: If Army X is force multiplying in three ways and Army Y is force multiplying in only two ways, the old way of looking at this through the mass lens would be a single (1) advantage—one more army, one

FORCE MULTIPLICATION

more soldier, or one more unit advantage. Simply put, X – Y or 3 – 2.

The Clausewitzian theory, however, states that Army X has a five-times advantage over Army Y because the advantage is squared.[41] By Army X force multiplying in three ways, that force is equal to nine forces. Army Y is force multiplying in only two ways, so their force is only equal to four. This creates a significant five-plus advantage for Army X.

$3^2 - 2^2 = 5$, the Clausewitz Advantage for Army X

So, in this example, Army X has a better, more innovative tactician as a leader and also has cuirassiers (heavy cavalry) and artillery. Army Y has only artillery and grenadiers (elite shock troops). The advantage to Army X is more than just the heavily armed cuirassiers individually. The advantage applied is factored. The speed, maneuverability, range, flexibility, combined arms, and reserves should be accounted for. This was Clausewitz's genius; he communicated the true advantage beyond just the individual masses.

The result: Force multiplication has an exponential effect on the outcome. As such, it's the antithesis of mass.

Mass sees only the numerical advantage of a force, not the exponential advantage.

I've used that exponential effect throughout my career in my approach to marketing. More importantly, I've used this approach to communicate our strategy not only to our marketing teams but to our finance team, the C-suite, and investors.

Let's apply the Clausewitz formula to a marketing plan. You can spend $1 million on the Yellow Pages, and you'll get that one ad, nothing more. But with force multiplication, you can spend that same money on one thing but generate a diverse set of assets. That same $1 million wasn't just going to get a new website; it was going to get content on that website that we could force multiply into additional assets.

As an example, if I need a blog post, why not multiply it with the following?

- **More Blog Content:** Make it a little longer by adding the byline and quotes from staff.
- **Podcast:** That blog piece becomes the basis for an interview with the staff you quoted for the article. Record the interview and use the content as a podcast.
- **Social Media Shares:** Take still images during the podcast session to share socially on multiple platforms, especially Facebook, Instagram, LinkedIn, and TikTok.
- **YouTube Videos:** While you're recording the podcast interviews, roll the video to create a

long-format video that can also be segmented into multiple shorter format pieces.
- **Business Development Literature:** Your boots on the ground will love material created from this blog post along with the photos.
- **Email:** Your business development team will be able to take the article, the videos, and the podcasts to create content-rich email blasts tailored to their audience.
- **Alumni Newsletter:** The blog article, video, and podcast are mentioned along with the call to action to interact with the content. The interaction request is more likely to be followed through on by your most ardent and passionate fans: your alumni.

If my competitor has similar content but features it only on their website and in an email blast, my advantage is 62 − 22 = 32. And the expense is now shared among six channels versus one, making it more affordable because the return on that smaller investment is easier to maximize.

If your team's ability to capture and process the leads is mature, you'll likely find your cost advantage in line with your force multiplication number.

> The attack upon one and the same body from several quarters is generally more effectual and decisive, the smaller this body is, the nearer it approaches to the lowest limit—that of a single combatant. An army can easily give battle on several sides, a division less easily, a battalion only when formed in mass, a single man not at all.
> —Carl von Clausewitz[42]

The C-suite bought into the idea but didn't give me the full $1 million from the Yellow Pages budget. They weren't ready to do that, but they gave me enough to hire a videographer and a web developer, and I could get going with the plan.

No One Wants to Pay for Unproven Innovation

Force multiplication itself isn't the innovation, but it allows you to innovate without driving up costs and to see success across numerous channels, which means you get buy-in on the innovation.

We weren't innovating at Foundations because we were trying to be cool. We had a strategy facilitated by force multiplication that allowed us to spread innovation costs across different budgets. It went like this:

1. We had the idea to launch a podcast.

2. We identified other areas of the business that could benefit from the podcast.
3. We proposed a percentage that the business development and HR budgets could contribute to the podcast team and setup.

By spreading the cost across a few different department budgets, the finance team wasn't freaked out that we were spending this huge amount on a marketing podcast.

Say you've already invested in building a video team and all the resources that go with it. Why not offer to deploy that to employee engagement? On Glassdoor.com, former employees write either positive or negative things about your company. As a marketing leader, I'm asking human resources to put some of their budget into marketing because these assets will help HR with recruiting. When we're interviewing clinical staff for a podcast, that's going to help the human resources team share the message, "Look at the great staff we have and how we're investing in our people!"

Of course, HR may push back and ask, "Why can't marketing just do it?"

I always responded, "Well, there's a cost to it, and if you want them to do it, it must have value for you." And we're not asking HR to create their own podcasts. We'll do it for them, but they do need to have some skin in the game, and the budget they allocate allows us to offset the costs of one thing (video content production).

Using force multiplication, we built a platform that housed video, podcasting, editors, content writers, social media, SEO, SEM, graphic design, alumni relations, and data analysis—and they all supported our clinical teams, business development, HR, and recruiting.

One of the largest benefits of this approach is how you communicate your overall marketing strategy to other members of the C-suite.

I was at a conference a few years back, and the speaker, who was delivering a marketing presentation, was asked how to measure the value of social media when experiencing pushback from finance.

He responded, "Ask the CFO how they measure the value of meeting times." That approach doesn't work with your partners on the finance side of the house.

Educating the finance corner of your office and aligning your strategy with their financial goals creates a positive synergy between your creative vision and their financial acumen. Having objective metrics tied to your financial goals gives you freedom of movement. If you're tracking all aspects of your marketing data, you're now in control and can make decisions objectively and decisively.

But how do you tie those metrics and get support before you've got the success to show for your methods?

FORCE MULTIPLICATION

That's precisely what force multiplication represents — a model to explain your actions.

When presenting my marketing ideas to the Foundations board, I did it using the force multiplication theory. I was a newbie CIO from a nontraditional background, but I had the conviction that these weren't just my opinions; I was mapping ideas following the strategic genius of Clausewitz.

This framing reduced risk for the company and the finance team supporting it. While they could quickly push back on the digital marketing ideas delivered by a young CIO, they weren't going to push back on an age-old military mental model.

The model gave my argument weight ... and some breathing room to implement innovation and build the team.

Then, the content started generating leads.

We gained momentum. Website traffic lifted, social media engagement grew, and YouTube subscribers rose. Most importantly, more and more potential patients started calling to request help for themselves or family members in need of a recovery program.

Within the year, I demonstrated that most of our inbound phone calls were now coming via the digital team, not the Yellow Pages. That gave me the evidence I needed to now support my request to redeploy some of our Yellow Pages advertising dollars into the digital lead engine, while still returning some of that spend back to the corporate bottom line.

Remember, I didn't come in demanding more money. I used this idea of force multiplication to start the process, and we accomplished more. We repurposed, redeployed, and built a monster engine.

We started seeing success; we tracked it, hooking marketing metrics to the finance team's goals, and that was the justification for us to hire more people and expand. We went from one videographer to two, then three. The business was growing, too, with more facilities added. When I started at Foundations, we were a marketing team of two. When I left, we had thirty.

We pushed the idea of force multiplication to all levels.

As an example, our copywriters had visions of grander things. Foundations is based in Nashville, so we had a lot of freelance musicians and aspiring creatives working for us, now writing SEO copy. That can be mind-numbing work for a creative.

Force multiplication made their job more interesting. It meant that they could add the fun stuff (photography, music, journalistic narrative) because I was able to force multiply it and spread the cost.

In behavioral health, if you want an article sitting as an anchor on your website, that article can typically be two thousand words long. Let's say I have a writer who wants to put together a piece on trauma, and they tell me, "Lee, I've got this idea, but it's going to be five thousand words." Maybe that becomes three pieces, and we break it up on the website. Suddenly, instead of just one long-format article, it becomes three pieces.

Then, the writer multiplies it further, saying, "These articles will also give us at least ten pull quotes we can use on social media over the next six months." Now, that one idea has become three articles and ten social media posts.

"But Lee," you might counter, "isn't this another example of mass? Isn't this quantity over quality?"

Remember, in the example of mass, the Romans had one soldier, and they had to figure out how to add more single soldiers to achieve a mass of thousands of individual soldiers. In force multiplication, we're not saying, "Go write twenty SEO articles." We're saying, "Go write one article, and apply force multiplication to see if you can do twenty things with it across multiple channels."

That's critical because, like many businesses, we were trying to promote Foundations as the solution for the problem people were seeking help for. Nobody was googling "Foundations Recovery Network." We wanted to be where our customers were, and we weren't going to pick one channel and say, "This is the only way you can find us." No, I wanted us to be present wherever our customers were. After all, they weren't looking for us; we were looking for them. So, we had to go find them.

Exponential Impact

Marketing can often seem like a random assortment of so many little things if you're only looking at each article, social media post, podcast, ad, and YouTube video in isolation. It's like looking at individual puzzle pieces: You can make out part of the image but not the whole. But when you start putting those piece together, something amazing happens. They become so much more together than they could ever be alone. The impact they make in unison is truly exponential.

People can do so many little things, but they don't think it's a big enough idea. "I'm only looking for a $1 million idea," you might argue. Maybe someday you'll get lucky and have one. I hope you do. But the truth is, it'd be a lot easier for most of us to come up with a solid $100,000 idea—and then apply it across ten different channels... or more.

That's the power of force multiplication.

WHAT NEXT?

 Apply this with your team.
Bring your videographer into your podcast interviews. Have only one camera? Get two. Cut up the B-roll footage for social media reels. Add other channels like TikTok. The cost is minimal, and you have already done the work on the podcast. Multiply that work!

 Apply this with your C-suite.
Document your strategy. Lay it out in a written document or presentation. Apply the strategy to your budget. Show how you're now engaged in numerous channels without breaking the bank.

 Gain a quick win.
Showcase a quick win, such as SEO traffic increases, inbound link increases, engagement with social, a successful new channel launch, and PR wins. Look for even small gains that can add to the momentum you are creating.

Chapter 5

WAR-GAMING

Growing up in the 1980s, I was exposed to the best movies of all time. Okay, I make that statement with a smile on my face, but who would disagree with such classics as *E.T.*, *Blade Runner*, *Rambo*, and *Animal House*? It was an amazing time to be in high school, seeing these movies every weekend.

The 1983 film *WarGames* starring Matthew Broderick and Ally Sheedy doesn't make everyone's top-movies list, but it stood out for me. It's a story of a teenager who hacks into America's nuclear defense system. The fictional AI asks Broderick's character if he would like to play a game, and the teen suggests playing "Global Thermonuclear War," not realizing how very real and dangerous this war game would turn out to be.

NEVER OUTMATCHED

Years later, while at Armor School, I studied and war-gamed on sand tables—our own version of computerized war-gaming. We moved model tanks and soldiers around, creating a visual of plans and opportunities that could unfold on the day of engagement.

War-gaming can be traced back to the Greeks, their abax table (sand table), and Archimedes's legendary death at the hands of Roman soldiers in 212 BCE. As the Romans approached, he is said to have exclaimed, "I beg of you, do not disturb this," while protecting the dust table with his circle drawings.[43]

Two thousand years later, a Prussian officer, Georg Heinrich Rudolf Johann von Reisswitz, took that concept several steps further with the first war-gaming exercise, *Kriegsspiel*, in the early 1800s to train Prussian army officers. Reisswitz was inspired by his father's military exercises and the desire to create a more realistic and systematic way to train officers and test military strategies.[44]

The game was played double-blind, meaning the players on either side could see what their opponents were doing only if they came into direct contact. It simulated actual battlefield conditions, including terrain, troop movements, and combat outcomes.

The rules were comprehensive, accounting for factors like morale and supply lines. A game master acted as an umpire, enforcing the rules and determining what a player could and couldn't observe. At the end of the game, the umpire's table was revealed, and the leaders offered a critique.

The Prussian army recognized the potential of *Kriegsspiel* as a training tool for its officers. In 1824, it was formally rolled out at *Kriegsakademie*, the Prussian "West Point," as part of their officer training program.

Kriegsspiel then spread beyond Prussia, influencing other European countries' military institutions. Different variations and adaptations of the game emerged, each with its own set of rules and objectives. In some cases, miniatures replaced wooden blocks, allowing for more detailed representations of troops. This encouraged officers to think critically, plan operations, and consider various factors that could affect the outcome of battles.

He who exercises no forethought but makes light of his opponents is sure to be captured by them.
—*Sun Tzu*[45]

The Fog of War

The concept of *fog of war*—not knowing what your opponent is doing—is a direct result of *Kriegsspiel*.

Planning for the fog of war is crucial in both military and nonmilitary contexts because it acknowledges the inherent uncertainty and unpredictability in complex, dynamic environments. The term *fog of war* describes the confusion, lack of information, and unpredictability that can occur during conflicts, crises, or rapidly changing situations.

Anticipating and planning for the fog of war has numerous advantages in helping leaders

WAR-GAMING

- deal with uncertainty,
- create a culture of flexibility,
- develop contingency plans,
- improve decision-making under stressful conditions,
- enhance resilience,
- highlight situational awareness,
- overcome overconfidence, and
- enhance communication.

In any operation, you rarely have perfect information. Planning for the fog of war means preparing for incomplete or misleading information. Rather than relying on a rigid, detailed plan that could fall apart when things change, leaders are encouraged to be adaptable, allowing quick shifts based on new information.

By acknowledging the fog of war, planners create multiple scenarios and fallback options to serve as contingency plans. This prevents a single point of failure and ensures that other viable options are available if one plan fails due to unforeseen circumstances.

While the fog of war makes perfect situational awareness impossible, simply being aware of the fog encourages constant reassessment of the situation. Leaders are more likely to seek out new information, adapt to changing realities, and make informed decisions on the fly.

A friend of mine works in marketing for a health and rehabilitation center. She recently toured one of their new facilities in Southern California. Inevitably, a competitor will open close by; that's just the nature of the health-care market. One center opens in the neighborhood, and a competitor shortly follows.

Right now, she's doing fine. Website traffic is good, ads are going great, and she's getting plenty of patient leads. But what happens when a competitor opens a neighboring facility? That ad she's been running at number one for months is now bumped down to two or three because the competitor is willing to spend more money. Leads are halved. What does she do?

The worst time to figure out the solution to that problem is after it happens. You panic when you suddenly lose half your leads and don't know how to replace them. And in that panicked state, you make bad decisions.

In 2017, Anthony J. Porcelli and Mauricio R. Delgado published "Stress and Decision Making: Effects on Valuation, Learning, and Risk Taking," teaching us that "When under stress, cognitive resources are diverted towards threat management, reducing the capacity for complex decision-making and biasing behavior towards simpler, heuristic-driven choices."[46]

Stress is going to bias your decision-making. You'll be limiting your potential responses and ability to overcome the situation without even realizing it. You'll miss opportunities to restrict losses and may also miss opportunities to advance or win. The alternative is to war-game situations before they happen; embracing this kind of planning will reduce your level of stress because you will have seen this situation or something like it before.

How Do You War-Game in Marketing?

In the military, the Fort Knox library provided training and lessons from past battles. My training focused on the European theater, but today's threats focus more on past battles in the Middle East and Asia. During training we'd take those previous examples and plot out the worst-case scenarios in the situations we were most likely to encounter.

This approach is universal.

Whether you're in the behavioral health, automotive, or technology industry, you can look to the past for the business horror stories that have wreaked havoc. Introduce those stories to your current team and war-game the possible solutions.

Your marketing leader can serve as games master. For scenario ideas, you can also include other departments that are dependent on marketing, like human resources or finance.

Examples we've gamed out include running a television ad:

- What happens if they put the wrong 800 number on your ad?
- What if your website goes down?
- What happens if you lose HubSpot connectivity?
- What happens if your Google Ads payment method expires?
- What happens if a competitor launches aggressive Google Ads campaigns?

These problems range in scale and impact, but it helps to consider how you would approach them before the actual event in every scenario.

As a marketing leader, a great starting point for coming up with war-gaming examples is to run through all the things that are working right now. Do that at a macro scale (we're hitting our inbound lead target every month), then do it at a micro scale (cost per lead is $2.50 through Google Ads). Now, start creating scenarios where those things are no longer working. What do you do if the cost per acquisition through Google Ads is suddenly no longer profitable? Or if that decline happens slowly over six months, what do you do then?

Then you start applying these scenarios to different areas of marketing planning. There are six of them:

Marketing Area #1: Strategy

You're not war-gaming in a vacuum; you're doing it with the whole marketing team because the best ideas don't always come from leadership.

Getting different minds together from various backgrounds will provide different perspectives and angles. Let's say you have an SEO problem. Traffic has dropped month on month over the past two quarters. The SEO manager will have some technical ideas, maybe a hypothesis on why the latest Google algorithm update is punishing our site, and some suggestions on what we need to change to get back on the right side of the algorithm.

The social media manager in the room might present a social media solution to an SEO problem. Maybe Google is placing greater importance on links and conversations happening around your brand on LinkedIn, which means you need to introduce new LinkedIn activities to earn those links on social media and improve your SEO traffic.

This is why everybody on the marketing team needs to be involved.

Occasionally, inviting people from outside marketing is also a great idea. Finance, for example, holds the keys to the marketing budget. As a marketing leader, you want to get those folks involved in the war-gaming aspects that could include pulling levers that impact budgets.

When you invite the CFO or head of HR into your war-gaming, the added bonus is that you come across as a serious player. Other departments start to see how methodical and strategic you are. When you need their help, such as when presenting to the C-suite, that reputation you develop for yourself will help you sell and defend your ideas. And if members of the finance team are a part of the war-gaming and that scenario comes to fruition, they're much more likely to sign off on your plans because they were part of developing them.

Marketing Area #2: Competitive Analysis

So often, we get tunnel vision with our business and fail to pay attention to some of the new upstarts. I think about Blockbuster and how they were very tunneled with their whole mass concept, which we discussed earlier. Then Netflix came along and started eating their lunch.

War-gaming forces you to look at the competitive landscape regularly. If you're war-gaming every six months, you'll push yourself to investigate any new players or competitors. If you don't do this, you might go a couple of years without researching competitors, and then a smaller company that had been quietly growing in your periphery suddenly mushrooms on you, catching you flat-footed.

I don't know whether Blockbuster did war-gaming, but if they did, they weren't doing it effectively. They certainly didn't war-game a scenario like, "What if a movie rental service pops up and starts offering a near-frictionless vending machine?" or "What if an upstart begins attacking us on price by offering dirt-cheap rentals for something like $1?" If they had, they would have been ready for Redbox.

In 2000, Netflix was relatively small and still working out its financial footing. Reed Hastings, the cofounder of Netflix, approached Blockbuster with an offer to sell Netflix. They proposed that Netflix manage Blockbuster's online brand while Blockbuster took care of the in-store business. The price they asked for was $50 million.[47]

Blockbuster's executives didn't see the value in the online rental model then. They reportedly laughed at the offer and turned it down, confident their physical stores were the future. They simply didn't anticipate how quickly the industry would shift toward digital.

What if they'd war-gamed and asked themselves, "What happens if people can instantly stream movies to their homes via the Internet?" Running through the possible outcomes, a $50 million investment in Netflix would have become a smart hedge.

Marketing Area #3: Resource Allocation

It's one thing to war-game, as Blockbuster might have done, a scenario like this: "We see this threat coming, so we should create our own streaming service." But who's actually going to do the work? You've got to at least define, in the beginning, who's going to execute. That's where war-gaming helps the leader understand. We might know the solution, but can we staff it?

Staffing is always a big issue in many companies. Nobody wants to be overstaffed and saddled with increased wages and inefficiencies related to idle time, duplicated tasks, and employee confusion about their roles. These all lead to a drag on earnings and an inability to use those resources to scale up. War-gaming allows you to play out staffing models. Are there people in other areas who can jump in to help in a crisis or an emergency?

There are many examples in war where support personnel like cooks, mechanics, and even administration were converted to riflemen in a time of need. Toward the end of World War II, the German forces launched a surprise attack near the Ardennes Forest that became known as the Battle of the Bulge. The Allies were initially unprepared for the assault and caught by surprise, which led to desperate measures to reinforce their lines. A winter storm was in full force, which eliminated air support and reconnaissance, and the Christmas holiday also contributed to a sense of respite by the Allies.

As the situation became critical, US commanders ordered that noncombat personnel, including cooks, clerks, and other support staff, be armed and sent to the front lines to help defend against the advancing German troops. These soldiers, who were not trained initially or equipped for frontline combat, were hastily given rifles and sent to fight alongside the infantry. They helped slow the German advance, which gave Gen. George Patton's forces time to arrive from the eastern part of France. Despite the initial chaos and lack of proper combat training, these men held the line until reinforcements arrived.

Similarly, Joseph Stalin declared a state of emergency as the Germans advanced on Moscow. Factory workers, clerks, and civilians were armed and hastily formed into defensive militias to defend Moscow. While often improvised, these contributions were critical to preventing a collapse and buying time for fully trained reinforcements.

How about your team? Are they all ready to answer phones, write content, mail letters, and answer online queries?

Let's say you have to shift gears. Suddenly, your YouTube channel is failing, so you decide to shift everything into Google Ads. Are the people handling your YouTube channel cross-trained in Google Ads? If you say you need to shift resources to Google Ads but you don't have anybody to do it, it's worthless.

I had a client with an in-house videographer who came from a television background. One of the opportunities we identified was having drone footage of the campus. The videographer had the editing and equipment knowledge; now he needed to go through the process of becoming certified and of identifying the required equipment. It would never be his full-time job, but what an opportunity to grow personally and plug a potential hole—having him certified and ready to go when the time came versus doing nothing and wishing that resource were immediately available.

Marketing Area #4: Crisis Management

We often war-game potential "crises" at Foundations Recovery Network and The Meadows. Nothing creates a crisis quite like a member of your board of directors reading a negative review on Google or Yelp. At Foundations, we worked with a husband-and-wife team, Rory and AJ Vaden, revamping our admissions center training. They encouraged our admissions center team to develop robust, well-documented, and personalized processes and training programs. I subsequently developed the DRAW model for responding to reviews that was aligned with their training:

D - Discover
R - Research
A - Answer
W - Work It Out

WAR-GAMING

Since it was part of our war-gaming, our team knew, once we discovered a negative review, what the order of attack was in trying to resolve it.

First, we *discover*: We monitored Google, Yahoo, Yelp, and Glassdoor for company reviews. Second, once we discover them, we *research* them. Are they legit? Did they receive service? Third, we have to *answer* the review. You can't just let it sit out there with no answer. And your answer may be very innocuous. It may not resolve an issue, but you need to acknowledge online that you're researching and looking into it. Then, the fourth job is the most crucial part: We have to *work it out*.

Here's an example:

When a woman's son came in for treatment at one of our California facilities, he showed up with two pieces of luggage. Our admissions policy, documented on our packing list, was that we allowed patients only one piece of luggage. It wasn't uncommon for patients to arrive and overlook that information, so a closet was used to store any extra bags. Our center let him put one piece of luggage in his room, and the other was locked in the storage closet. At least that's what they said.

Thirty days later, when he was graduating, his second bag was gone, lost. According to the mom, it was a Louis Vuitton bag. So, when the son returned home, she asked him, "Where's my Louis Vuitton bag?"

"They lost it."

She called the facility numerous times, was transferred to different offices, left messages for the clinical director and the patient care coordinator, called the Nashville admissions center, and spoke to staff in housekeeping. Nobody returned her call or had any answers as to the location of the bag. After a couple of weeks, she was flummoxed and finally wrote a one-star review.

Our team in Nashville saw it and jumped into action. We confirmed the patient's status. Yep, her son was with us. I personally called the mom, introduced myself, and asked how we could help. I listened to her story, made notes, and committed to finding a solution. She offered to send us a receipt. She did everything right, but she was just mad that nobody was calling her back. That was her big gripe: No one was returning her calls.

I contacted the facility CEO and said, "Listen, here's what happened. Y'all lost it. I think we need to reimburse her." We ended up writing her a check for twelve hundred dollars, no strings attached. She got the check. The next day, her one-star review was edited to a five-star review.

That's working it out.

Her son had a great experience and returned to his family to continue his recovery. The CEO took action regarding the center's mistake in handling the luggage, and they adopted new luggage control processes. All these positive outcomes were realized because we were prepared.

And that process all came from war-gaming.

You could put plenty of potential crisis management situations through war-gaming, some much more severe than negative customer reviews. What happens if you have a data breach? As a marketing lead, you'll have to get involved from a press perspective. What's the press release going to say? Which law firm are you going to hire? You may not know what to do throughout the entire process. Things morph. But it helps to understand the first few steps so that you're not reacting to the situation for the first time under stress.

Marketing Area #5: Team Collaboration, Learning, and Training

At Foundations Recovery Network, our marketing team grew from three to thirty people over my decade as lead, but only some work together daily. When you're war-gaming, you're getting all the different groups together—print, conference, business development, digital video, social media, alumni, SEO, web development, and content. Everybody appreciated the collaboration and saw how vital their contribution could be in a crisis that, on the surface, may not seem to involve them.

You're also exposed to areas where you need to do further training. Or other skills you need to gather. Or an attitude you need to adopt.

The four national conferences we put on each year as part of our marketing approach are another example of our use of force multiplication at Foundations. Our conference lineup for several years included

1. Moments of Change at The Breakers in West Palm Beach, Florida
2. Innovations in Recovery at the Hotel Del Coronado in San Diego, California
3. Recovery Results at The Ritz Carlton Hotel, Dallas, Texas
4. Innovations in Behavioral Health at The Downtown Hilton, Nashville, Tennessee

These conferences allowed us to showcase our staff and outcomes and to connect with like-minded behavioral health companies. They were also asset-generating machines in terms of content. We developed some of our best authoritative content at our conferences from interviews for articles, podcast and YouTube interviews, social media content, HR recruiting, and promoting our Heroes in Recovery social movement.

Ahead of these events, we had to war-game hosting a conference with more than two thousand attendees. The planning and preparation that our conference director, Jenny Decker, led us through was extensive. What happens if a hurricane approaches West Palm Beach? What do we do if a keynote speaker is late or sick? What do we do if there is a hotel workers' strike? How do we handle a hotel room snafu that happens with a VIP? What do we do if protestors show up?

Handing the reins to young leaders like Jenny to guide us through critical planning was crucial in developing the next layer of leaders and in serving as a model for the type of collaboration that war-gaming can bring to a team.

In war there is no substitute for experience, no substitute for the intuitive skill that comes from repeated practice.
—Col. John F. Schmitt[48]

Marketing Area #6: Documentation and Urgency

You have only so many hours in a week to dedicate to your work efforts. So, any hours dedicated to war-gaming need to be valued. You want the work and decisions made to be readily accessible when similar situations arise. You may have war-gamed the scenario a year ago, and it's now suddenly starting to play out. You're going to dust that scenario off and run through it. You may have some adjustments to make, but you've already war-gamed most of it. If you don't document it, you may be working from a faulty memory, or essential team members may have left or are unavailable.

With this documentation, your whole team knows what needs to happen when they're most stressed, and the CFO and the CEO will love knowing that. They can sit back and relax, saying, "Okay, we've just heard that a new treatment center is open, but you've already war-gamed the scenario. Here's what we're going to do. We've documented a response; this is the tactic we'll start with." So, you're not paralyzed, you're not spending days or weeks trying to figure it out; you've already thought about it.

And calling it war-gaming creates a sense of urgency. A lot of these military principles are based on literal life-and-death situations. Not to be overly dramatic, but you're going to go through many challenges that could be life-and-death situations for your company. Sometimes, we're too soft with the work we're doing internally, but this is serious business. When you treat it as such, the people responsible for the tasks at hand feel the gravity of it.

WAR-GAMING

WHAT NEXT?

 Apply this with your team.
To get started, host a war-gaming session with your team and actually title it *War-Gaming*. (You'll get a lot of messages about what is going on.) Start small with two or three scenarios. Keep the meeting tight and no more than thirty to forty-five minutes.

 Apply this with your C-suite.
Report on your outcomes of you first war-gaming session. Request one other department to join your exercise next month or next quarter.

 Gain a quick win.
Be alert for when one of your scenarios happens and report it when it does. Share that with the team and C-suite. Document and include it in your marketing plan and see if your compliance or training department would also be interested in having this information.

Chapter 6

ANVIL AND HAMMER

When I hear "anvil and hammer," I can't help but envision a blacksmith working a horseshoe. However, in military parlance, those words conjure a different meaning.

The *anvil and hammer* tactic is a maneuver that involves using two forces to encircle and crush an enemy formation. The *anvil* represents a stationary force that engages the enemy and holds them in place. Simultaneously, the *hammer* is a mobile force that maneuvers to attack the enemy from the flank or rear, exploiting weaknesses created by the anvil's engagement.

You may use some of your troops, artillery, or drones to keep the enemy busy while you give your light infantry or armored cavalry time to engage the flanks or encircle. As the commander, you're not expecting to win in the middle suddenly. You know you'll win on the flanks, but you've got to give your team time to come around on the flanks. That's a typical example of the anvil and hammer. Numerous variations of this concept have been used throughout history and into modern times.

The Military Origin of the Anvil and Hammer

One of the best examples of this strategy in ancient times is from the reign of Philip II. He turned the backwater state of Macedon (later Macedonia) into a formidable force that conquered Greece and built the war machine that his son, Alexander the Great, inherited.

Philip professionalized soldiering in Macedon, allowing his state to have an army that regularly drilled and created new tactics. He turned a group of wealthy nobles' sons and their horses into a feared calvary unit, innovating this unit to ride in wedge formation versus the typical abreast formation of the time.

In the Battle of Chaeronea, Philip II used the anvil-and-hammer tactic to great effect. Located in central Greece, near Delphi, Chaeronea was the scene of many conflicts in antiquity. Philip II and his Macedonian forces faced a coalition of Greek city-states led by Athens and Thebes.

Philip positioned his phalanx in the center of his line, armed them with the newly innovated *sarissas* (a long spear), and tasked them with holding the

ANVIL AND HAMMER

Greeks in place and not giving up ground in the middle. Philip's new sarissa was longer than the typical Greek spear, allowing the Macedonians to inflict damage from farther away in battle.[49] This was the anvil, holding the Greek soldiers in place, not trying to win the battle outright in the middle by themselves but engaging and keeping the Greeks focused on the center.

Meanwhile, Philip's son, Alexander, was a rising young Macedonian army commander tasked with swinging the hammer. In this case, Alexander's cavalry charged in, targeting the Greek flank. He caught the Greeks in the middle where they could not react to what was approaching. The Greek forces couldn't turn quickly enough to face Alexander's charging cavalry. The soon-to-be Alexander the Great used this tactic throughout his battles in Asia, and this victory led to Macedonian dominance over the Greek city-states. It was one of the best examples of the anvil and hammer tactic in antiquity.[50]

---- ★ ----

You must either conquer and rule or serve and lose, suffer or triumph, be the anvil or the hammer.
—Johann Wolfgang von Goethe[51]

---- ★ ----

This military strategy has endured for two millennia. One of the best examples in modern times is from the Gulf War in 1991, during Operation Desert Storm. The US and coalition partner forces created a defensive line in northern Saudi Arabia to commit the Iraqi troops to engage and face off the Americans. This defensive line was the anvil. After weeks of bombardment, Gen. Norman Schwarzkopf launched his "left hook," his hammer. US and coalition forces came sweeping into southern Iraq from the west, effectively cutting off and enveloping many Iraqi troops in Kuwait and southern Iraq. This tactic was one of the factors in the quick and decisive coalition victory.[52]

★

Do what is right, not what you think the high headquarters wants or what you think will make you look good.
—*Gen. Norman Schwarzkopf*[53]

★

Marketing Lessons from the Anvil and Hammer

In marketing, there are times when you have to engage your competition with one tactic in order to give your other tactics time to work for your overall strategy. For example, you could launch a paid search campaign to give your search engine optimization time to build. Your overall strategy might be to win at search engine

ANVIL AND HAMMER

optimization (SEO), but the paid search can hold your competition to the anvil while your SEO hammer moves into position.

Let's say your potential customers are searching online, but you're not visible organically yet. Your SEO isn't there right now because you're just starting—your product or facility is new. So, you go after that customer with paid search. Your competitor, which has an SEO presence, is going to see you appear all of a sudden in a paid search ad showing up at the top of the page. They're going to have to put resources toward reacting now and will have to start thinking about increasing their paid-search budget.

You've identified how you want to win this battle through organic search, but it'll take time to get your troops together to locate where you need to go. If you don't engage in the battle to win that customer today, your competitor wins that customer and every one that follows. In that case, they'll strengthen their position because they'll win everything, and their revenue will continue to grow.

With marketing, you're expecting some kind of revenue to come in. There are very few times when your company will give you millions of dollars to build up your SEO without anything coming back. So, starting your paid search allows you to go after those customers immediately while building up your strategy.

NEVER OUTMATCHED

How *The New York Times* Used Wordle as an Anvil

During the COVID-19 pandemic, software developer Josh Wardle started tinkering with an online word game concept. By October 2021, he had a fully functional word game that involved solving five-letter words in six guesses or fewer. The game, Wordle, was an instant hit. Millions of fans flocked to the site to play daily. Stats and sharing with friends allowed this concept to go viral quickly. Wardle sold the game to The *New York Times* four months later for a reported seven-figure payday.

The *Times* did something clever here. They could have added access to their subscription model for their daily newspaper or created a new gaming subscription just for the game. They could have used Wordle itself to try to recoup the money they paid for Wordle and to profit. But they're not in the online gaming business. They applied the anvil and the hammer. They bought Wordle and used it as the anvil in the fight for subscribers.

The game remained free and moved into the *Times*' game section. They migrated the game to maintain users' access to their stats and daily streaks. Now, the Wordle users were part of the *Times* ecosystem, where they engaged in other *Times* games and, most importantly, were exposed to *Times*' digital subscription opportunities.

ANVIL AND HAMMER

The *Times* didn't buy Wordle to win the digital subscriber battle. Wordle holds the center, keeping potential subscribers engaged with the *Times* so their hammers can convert bundled offers. They deployed their marketing cavalry to convert these millions of Wordle fans, and by acquiring Wordle, they also created a situation where competitors now had to invest money and resources to respond to Wordle's success. Competitors withdrew from "active battle" against the *Times*' digital subscription cavalry and spent engaging the *Times*' anvil, Wordle, which was drawing attention through free gaming.

This strategy has been so successful that *The New York Times* developed two other wildly successful games — Connections, launched in 2023, and Strands, launched in 2024. When one online game becomes dated and viral engagement declines, they launch something else to stay engaged. These games are all free. They know their purpose: Hold the center; stay engaged.

Psychology Today: A Print Anvil in a Digital World

Another example from my time working in behavioral health is *Psychology Today*, founded in 1967 by psychologist and entrepreneur Nicholas Charney at a time when public interest in psychology was growing rapidly.

The magazine made concepts in psychology accessible to the general public by translating academic research into digestible articles. As the magazine gained readership, it became a staple of medical office waiting rooms and expanded into a wider range of psychological topics like self-improvement, parenting, and mental health challenges.

In the 1980s, Charney sold *Psychology Today* to the American Psychological Association, which later sold it to private investors. These changes pushed the magazine into even more contemporary topics like relationships, career concerns, and the challenges of everyday modern life.

By 2000, *Psychology Today*, like many print publications, was facing a decline in subscribers and advertisers. They prepared and successfully launched their website, PsychologyToday.com. One of the key elements of the site was its therapist directory, which has become one of the top tools for finding qualified mental health professionals. While many websites like Rehab.com and Recovery.com have tried to scrape content from the Internet to build marketing directories, *Psychology Today* has maintained its advantage through quality and authority, exemplified by its multiformat publishing. Therapists and treatment centers maintain their listings, credentials, licensing, photos, and videos, giving them access to the digital marketplace powered by search engines.

During this shift to digital, *Psychology Today* has continued to publish print editions bimonthly. They could have discontinued their print editions, but print continues to separate them competitively as their digital competitors seem single-threaded. It's their anvil.

Their print publication still appears in subscribers' mailboxes, health-care offices, and magazine racks and is still delivered to professionals and policy wonks nationwide. They maintain their capability in print because no other online competitor offers that option. Their content has contributed to the destigmatization of mental health and addiction conversations, and their articles are appealing to and written by both professionals and popular media.

Pushing Back on the Pushback

Anvils like Wordle and *Psychology Today*'s print edition feed into hammer activities that directly pull in leads and sales. But while you, the marketer, know this to be true, you will receive pushback from others in the business when you implement your anvil.

CFO: "You're asking me to spend money on something that *may not be* the winning strategy?"

Marketing: "Yes, I'm suggesting the business spend money on more expensive auction-driven paid ads because we'll hold our opponent there while this other, more cost-effective marketing strategy, SEO, will come in and win."

That's a tough concept for accounting or finance departments to embrace, because they don't like spending money. Their objective is to drive down costs and maximize profit. They don't like the paid search landscape, which can be volatile and expensive depending on the competition.

Typically, when you tell the C-suite that you're going to spend money in a place where you're not expecting to win long-term, their answer is, "Well, don't spend it." But not everything you spend on marketing will convert at the same percentage or at all. Some marketing tactics, the anvils, don't convert, and that's not their job. They have to work in tandem with the hammer that does convert.

From 2008 to 2018, directory listing websites in the treatment center industry represented some of the top producers of leads to treatment centers for potential patients. These directory sites were built to take advantage of how search engine algorithms worked. They comprised thousands of pages of treatment centers and affiliated services, listed with addresses and basic descriptions along with generic content built on keyword-friendly domain names like Rehab.com and Recovery.com.

Treatment centers rushed in to advertise and buy the patient leads these sites were generating—lots of people clambering to swing that hammer, shifting marketing spend to what they perceived was cheaper and easier. These centers stopped investing in their own SEO or content, their anvils. And, for a few years, the tactic worked (for some). Then Google, under pressure from ethical marketing advocates and members of the United States Congress, implemented a number of algorithm changes and LegitScript certification for advertisers in behavioral health.

In July 2018, the US House Energy and Commerce Subcommittee on Oversight and Investigations held a hearing titled "Examining Advertising and Marketing Practices within the Substance Use Treatment Industry." During this session, industry leaders discussed the ethical concerns surrounding paid search advertising in behavioral health. Mark Mishek, president and CEO of the Hazelden Betty Ford Foundation, emphasized the need for quality standards and regulatory frameworks:

> Most in our field do great work. But to ensure ethical, quality care for all who seek help for addiction, we believe it is time to establish quality standards and a consistent, enforceable regulatory framework for the addiction treatment industry. The stakes—patient safety and public confidence in addiction treatment—are high.[54]

This testimony highlighted the industry's commitment to ethical advertising practices and the importance of maintaining public trust in behavioral health services.

Additionally, the National Association of Addiction Treatment Providers (NAATP) updated its code of ethics to prohibit the buying or selling of leads. This addressed concerns that some treatment centers were acquiring leads from middlemen operating generic websites. These sites often did not disclose their affiliations, leading to potential patient misdirection.

Overnight, these website rankings disappeared from the first page, and they were not able to bid in the paid search auctions. The treatment centers that relied on these hammers were suddenly left without access to digital marketing–generated leads.

Marketing can be fragmented. It's not always easy to measure what's contributing. Some of the stuff you're doing on social, for example, may be contributing, even though you can't tie a conversion to it. And if you pull that anvil, suddenly, the hammer no longer works either.

Many people who don't work in marketing want to look at all marketing initiatives, select the cheapest, and eliminate the others. The military understands that each component of a plan cannot necessarily be stripped and successfully applied in isolation; a tactic may not be the primary goal, but it's just as critical to the battle's outcome. When you explain this mental model, the tide shifts, and your team and leadership will begin to understand that this supports the strategy. It looks like all the results are coming from the hammer, but you can't pull the anvil. It's part of the system.

But ... how do you know the anvil is working?

Is the enemy committing resources to attacking your anvil? Is their marketing effort starting to tire, to lose consistency or effectiveness? You may see fewer articles posted or less activity shared on social media, or maybe the quality of the assets they create is slipping. These can be signs that your anvil is holding its position and doing its job from a marketing perspective.

Podcasting Is the Modern Marketing Example of an Anvil

Cumberland Heights is a marketing consulting client of mine in Nashville. Founded in 1966, it is the oldest residential treatment center in Tennessee. I've been around Cumberland Heights since I joined Foundations in 2008. We were friendly competitors and mutually respected each other's work in the space. Jay Crosson, the CEO, invited me to breakfast in August 2022.

I started my engagement with them, diving deep into their operation and brand—interviewing, touring, and researching. They have an interesting story. A hundred-acre rural property was bought with the vision of changing recovery access from small groups, which were the primary access point in the 1940s and 1950s, to an approach where larger numbers of patients could access the twelve-step care on campus with housing, meals, and services all in one place.

Everyone knows about the Betty Ford Center, but Cumberland Heights has helped tens of thousands of people and has a sixty-year history. Still, nobody knows them outside of Tennessee. Everyone in health care knows a little of the backstory of Healthcare Corporation of America (HCA), founded by Tommy Frist Sr., his son Tommy Frist Jr., and their business partner Jack Massey. Tommy Frist Sr. was one of the cofounders of Cumberland Heights back in 1966. What a pedigree!

We also needed to promote the tremendous clinical team they'd put together. The potential content from their sixty-plus years of experience and their professional clinical staff solves their lack of SEO presence. I told them, "I think you should consider creating a podcast."

Their initial response was, "I don't know about that. I don't know if that's our brand. Does it convert?"

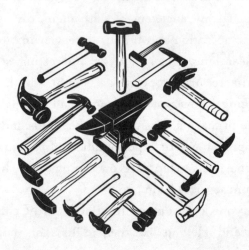

ANVIL AND HAMMER

I explained that they shouldn't worry about the patient conversion directly from the podcast. This is an anvil. The win would come from the industry authority they'd create and the relationships they'd enhance. The expense would be fully accounted for in the marketing budget but would have a different ROI. The conversions would appear in the business development, web, and alumni admissions lift.

Fast-forward a year into my consulting. I was at Cumberland Heights' annual fundraiser held at the Ryman Auditorium in Nashville. Their chief science officer, Nick Hayes, hosts their new podcast. Nick has come into his own hosting the podcast series and regularly interviews top thought leaders in behavioral health, alumni, and clinical staff.

Nick approached me at the event and said, "Lee, I just met a woman who put her son at Cumberland Heights, and it was because she listened to the podcast."

I smiled and said, "Ah, you invested in your anvil, and now you're sharing those podcasts on your website, social media, or through your alumni or business development relationships. You now have a hammer that's swinging away."

I'm not saying every marketing strategy or company will have a hammer and anvil, but it's a strategy to consider, and the explanation is key. In a marketing sense, the anvil can often be subtle. Everyone's looking at and celebrating the hammers such as the social media engagement and the business development events. A podcast or content can be an unsung hero in the hammer's success. And that success would not have happened without the anvil. The podcast and the SEO content derived from that podcast content are now giving your social media teams and your business development teams content and relationships to swing as hammers.

This works only if you celebrate the anvil.

Everybody wants to be the star quarterback or wide receiver. But you're not opening holes without the offensive line or plugging holes without the defensive line.

In marketing, social media is the sleek, innovative, and fun job, like the star quarterback. However, it might be that the content SEO person acting as the day in, day out anvil is the real star, like the offensive line. Without them, you won't be successful in some of these other things, and the team needs to understand they can't succeed without the anvil.

---- ★ ----

Those who know football know the game is won or lost in the trenches, along the line.
—Grey Ruegamer[55]

---- ★ ----

ANVIL AND HAMMER

This mental model helps everyone in the team understand the value of those other marketing components that don't always get the recognition they deserve.

Finding Your Anvil

You may be reading this thinking, *Oh, I see my problem. I've been stuck using the hammer, trying to win the battle with only the cavalry.* You may realize that you had an anvil and cut that expense, not realizing its importance to your overall success.

So, how do you find the anvil? I recommend two key steps:

First, *lay out the strategy*. Identify the supporting roles different marketing elements play in the overall strategy. Connecting these roles into a strategy and communicating their roles will help protect your marketing plans from being chopped up piecemeal as though the components operate entirely independently.

Second, *analyze the competition*. Figure out where you're behind. You'll need to be vulnerable and honest with yourself and eventually as an organization. Before making assumptions about what your hammers and anvils could be, find out what your competition is doing. They're already engaged in battle with you, probably eating your lunch in some areas. Look at their content and follow the trail: the length of the content, the people quoted in the content, the links derived from that content, the frequency of their content creation, the force multiplication they employ.

You may be using all these sexy tactics that could fall into the hammer category, but what are the items that may not be sexy? They may not be what's written about or talked about, but you know that that's what's underlying. Look at what your competitors are doing or what other people are doing outside your industry and try to figure out what they are doing that you're not seeing.

When you're trying to research how companies are getting the results you want, there are usually non-obvious things you need to dig into to say, "All right, I can see that they're doing X, Y, and Z, but those are obvious. Is there something here supporting this I'm not seeing?"

How do you recognize if you have an unbalanced strategy? When evaluating your marketing channels, you have to include not only the cost conversion but what support they give to your overall marketing effort. If you are only active with the lowest cost per acquisition, then you may be setting yourself up for a big surprise. In addition, are you encouraging your team to look to build anvils or are they under constant pressure for quick hammer wins?

Employing the anvil and hammer can give you a voice to communicate the larger picture that your marketing efforts are painting. Use it to unite all the important elements you are building.

WHAT NEXT?

 Apply this with your team.

Identify the parts of your marketing efforts that represent the anvils. What parts may have a slightly higher cost per lead or appear to the naked eye as less attention-grabbing?

Similarly, what are the elements of your strategy that are the hammer?

 Apply this with your C-suite.

Explain that this apparent marketing dichotomy is a synergistic marketing strategy. You need both efforts to win.

 Gain a quick win.

Celebrate the anvil, not just the hammer. Promoting the hammer is easy, but showcase the effort in building and holding your anvil. Highlight your SEO team in internal newsletters, and use a tool like Geckoboard to display anvil efforts like SEO article traffic or Google My Business phone calls/leads.

Chapter 7

INTELLIGENCE

For centuries, humans have relied on subjective, anecdotal, and historically biased data in the absence of objective data. Take, for instance, Queen Boudicca, the Iceni Celtic tribal leader who famously revolted against the Roman Empire in first-century Britain. As her forces destroyed numerous Roman settlements, including Londinium (present-day London), the Roman historian Cassius Dio documented her story. Dio portrays Boudicca as a fierce and inspiring leader. His descriptions of her height and piercing eyes create an image of her commanding presence. According to Dio, she wore a colorful tunic and a thick gold necklace and carried a spear, embodying her as the archetype of a warrior queen.[56]

He also writes that Boudicca employed a form of divination, which could be called heuristic decision-making

NEVER OUTMATCHED

today—making decisions based on rules of thumb or past experiences. Boudicca would release a hare from the folds of her dress and interpret the direction it ran to guide her army. That sounds strange to most of us today, but how often do you experience leaders or coworkers following their "gut instincts" or practicing intuitive decision-making? Are you relying on data or releasing rabbits to decide what to do?

This lack of data-driven decision-making always pushes armies back to what they could see: mass. As we saw in chapter 4, combat was mainly large groups of individuals fighting almost one-on-one. As one soldier fell wounded, exhausted, or killed, the next rank behind them would fill in and battle the opposing soldier.

Change and innovation started moving quickly in ancient times as societies connected through trade and competition. Today, our businesses and services are impacted by seemingly unconnected models. Now, ride-sharing services deliver our favorite restaurant food, which leads to ghost kitchens being set up to meet the new demand. Advancements in one area can quickly disrupt whole new markets.

In ancient societies, military advancement was often pushed through an external catalyst that accelerated the push to change and survive. Why do some succeed and some fail in riding these waves of innovation? Intelligence offers a clue.

Hannibal or Paullus and Varro?

The Battle of Cannae, fought on August 2, 216 BCE, was one of the most significant engagements of the Second Punic War between Rome and Carthage. It took place near the town of Cannae in southeastern Italy.

Hannibal—not to be confused with the meticulous serial killer in *Silence of the Lambs*—was the Carthaginian general well known for his invasion of Italy through his treacherous crossing of the seemingly impenetrable Alps. His forces inflicted several defeats on the Romans for the first time on their native soil. How does this military genius who lived more than two thousand years ago inform modern-day approaches to marketing?

At the Battle of Cannae, the Roman forces were led by experienced consuls Lucius Aemilius Paullus and Gaius Terentius Varro. The Roman army numbered

NEVER OUTMATCHED

between eighty and ninety thousand troops, while the Carthaginians presented only about fifty thousand. Both armies included traditional infantry or foot soldiers along with cavalry. Hannibal even had a few war elephants among his cavalry that had survived the Alps crossing.

The Romans approached the battle from a position of dominant mass and opted for a confrontation with the Carthaginians. They arranged their mass in a traditional formation with their infantry aligned in the center and their cavalry deployed to their flanks.

Hannibal knew he was outnumbered and couldn't win in a war of attrition. He had to be innovative and act on the intelligence he was gathering on his adversaries. Hannibal understood Roman tactics well, and his forces had scouted the battlefield terrain. He subsequently devised a tactical plan that positioned his troops in a concave formation. Hannibal deployed his newest, less experienced troops in the center and his most disciplined and experienced African infantry and Gaelic mercenaries on the flanks. Meanwhile, he positioned his cavalry in reserve to the rear.

As the horns blared and the battle flags signaled for Roman units to move forward, Hannibal's center, comprising his weaker forces, slowly gave up ground to their opposing and better-matched Roman units. However, this seeming weakness drew the Romans into Hannibal's trap. As the initial moments of the battle

INTELLIGENCE

unfurled, the Carthaginian cavalry was released to engage their counterparts and attack the rear echelons of the Roman forces, neutralizing the Roman cavalry. Remember the anvil and the hammer? Hannibal's deceptive anvil is a classic example. The Carthaginians had effectively encircled the Roman troops, which were now under pressure from all sides.

The Romans were trapped in a pocket that was becoming tightly packed. Hannibal's experienced units now supported the weaker Carthaginian forces and were systematically slaughtering the trapped Roman soldiers, who were so crammed together that they could not maneuver even to turn and face attacks from the rear.

History documents that fifty to seventy thousand Roman soldiers were killed, including both consuls. The defeat was a severe blow to Rome at the time and

is recorded as one of the most decisive victories in military history.

The Battle of Cannae demonstrated Hannibal's tactical genius and remains a classic example of a double-envelopment maneuver. It was planned based on his intimate knowledge, which he derived from the great intelligence gathered about his enemy.

Many times, when I have been engaged in consulting on marketing by a CEO or CMO, the conversation begins in a financial context. "How much are we spending? What is the cost per lead or acquisition? What is the number of full-time employees (FTEs)?" These types of conversations usually point to a team or a company relying on old battlefield tactics of mass. These business leaders ask, "How much money can we throw at the problem?" or "How much staff deploy to fix this?" They are probably positioned like Paullus and Varro, looking at their dominant mass of resources and staff and thinking, *I cannot lose.*

However, when considering your marketing strategy, you need to instead ask the question Paullus and Varro did not: "What intelligence have we gathered?"

Then, take it a little further. What intelligence have you shared with your teams or departments? Do all the departments know their role? Do they understand you are applying a double-envelopment maneuver or an oblique order of battle? Well, I'm

INTELLIGENCE

sure you wouldn't call your strategies by those names, but do they at least understand your vision and plan? Or are you just hiring salespeople, publishing blogs, and sharing photos?

Some of us work for large companies, such as Coca-Cola, HCA, and Apple—you know, the modern-day Carthaginians, Greeks, and Romans. But the rest of us represent small or mid-size businesses.

And yet we act like the Roman consuls, Paullus and Varro.

Mass makes it look like you're trying; your reports are filled with it. Can you imagine that day of the Battle of Cannae? Picture the Romans sitting there, outfitted in their finery, with flags flying, almost double the troops as the opposing army.

I'm sure they looked magnificent, the very image of success—until Hannibal's forces started tearing right through them. By the time the Romans realized what had happened, they had already lost.

They lost because they were a one-trick pony. Hannibal, on the other hand, gathered intelligence, crafted a plan, and deployed the orders effectively to outsmart the Romans and win.

★

Know the enemy and know yourself, and you can fight a hundred battles without disaster.
–Sun Tzu[57]

★

Intelligence Beats Mass

The absence of intelligence can breed inefficiency. In ancient battles, the lack of intelligence led to incorrect assumptions on troop placement, complacency about actions to expect, surprises in weather or terrain, and miscalculations about support needed, such as food, water, and ammunition.

I remember when one of my early consulting clients hired me to do a comprehensive marketing analysis. In the kickoff meeting, they mentioned that digital admissions were nonexistent but that they were very pleased with their social media campaigns. "Our social media posts are so beautiful," they said with beaming smiles. "They really match our brand."

As I looked into their channels more deeply, I saw hundreds of posts and only a handful of engagements. Of those interactions, many were likes, and the only shares were from staff.

I saw nothing driving significant traffic when I looked at the numbers and data. Search engine–optimized and paid search pages dwarfed the clicks they were getting from social media.

---- ★ ----

Social media is not about the exploitation of technology but service to community.
—Simon Mainwaring[58]

---- ★ ----

INTELLIGENCE

The social media manager and the agency stood there like Paullus and Varro. They looked good, had lots of posts, and received lots of praise from leadership. Before long, though, leadership will start asking the hard questions. The first should be, "What business results is this delivering?"

At some point, the battle ensues. A new CEO arrives, a board member asks questions, and investors want data. Now is the time to avoid the ego trap and gather your intelligence. Stop relying on old battle techniques like mass. Be Hannibal, or you'll be surprised one day when you lose your job.

Why Marketers Lean on Mass Rather Than Innovation

The advent of digital marketing gave us amazing data to look at and process. It's easy to become consumed by the mass—thousands of likes and hundreds of thousands of impressions—but what about the business, the revenue? Why are we sometimes powerless to gather intelligence or innovate in our roles in marketing?

Two factors can become overwhelming in business, especially for young or emerging leaders.

Loss Aversion

The psychological principle of *loss aversion* states that the emotional pain stemming from a loss is much greater than the pleasure that can be derived from gains. That is, all things being equal, most people would rather avoid a big loss than experience a big win. We sometimes reject investments in our business or marketing because we fear loss, even when the expected value is positive.

Status Quo Bias

The *status quo bias* in business is the tendency to oppose change and stick to the current way of doing things. This manifests in many ways, notably as resistance to adopting new technologies or processes for fear of disruption or inconvenience. These missed opportunities lead to stagnation in a business and offer competitors an opening to win by developing better transitions for consumers and new offerings.

There are numerous examples of loss aversion and status quo bias in war. One is the United States' continued involvement in Vietnam despite increasing casualties and declining public support. Leaders feared the perceived loss of credibility regarding the Cold War more than the tangible costs of continuing the war.

Or consider how Adolf Hitler insisted on holding Stalingrad at all costs during the Battle of Stalingrad. His decision was driven by the fear of losing prestige and control of territory the Germans had quickly overrun. The Germans faced encirclement and were ordered to fight to the last man, resulting in devastating losses.

How do we fight this resistance to change, this strategic inertia? We have to frame not only the opportunity cost but also diminishing outcomes. The status quo costs will keep piling up, and your return will diminish because the competition is not sitting still. Your competition is motivated and has a sense of urgency.

Use data to help counteract the emotional bias that lives in loss aversion and status quo. Small, incremental changes can help reduce institutional resistance.

Understand Your Opponent
In the army, the general staff is organized into a structure designed to handle various functional areas crucial to military operations. This structure is often known as the "G-Staff." Each section has a specific focus, and these sections are typically numbered G1 through G9:
- G-1: Personnel
- G-2: Intelligence
- G-3: Operations
- G-4: Logistics
- G-5: Plans
- G-6: Signal and Communications
- G-7: Training and Exercises
- G-8: Finance and Resource Management
- G-9: Civil-Military Operations

Hannibal understood his opponent. In the army, we would say he had good G-2. He understood the Roman tactics and was confident in how they would approach the battle.

We often employed good intelligence strategy at Foundations. We analyzed our competitors extensively. We studied American Addiction Centers, Acadia, UHS, Cliffside, and Betty Ford. We also examined the nonclinical groups that were heavily investing to sell phone calls and marketing services in our space. We had to compete not only with other treatment providers but also with marketing services companies.

We would reverse engineer their web strategies. We learned the optimal length of content, frequency, and quality, and most importantly, we figured out the long-tail keywords that were not being fought over. Let the other companies battle it out for the national keywords *alcohol rehab*; we'll own *new methods for treating alcoholism*, for example.

While understanding your opponent is crucial, you also need to understand that your opponent can change. What if Hannibal had simply *assumed* the Romans would act one way . . . but then the Romans suddenly had an unexpected innovative moment?

Your competitors will not always be myopic, so you need to understand what your competitors are doing. (This is where war-gaming comes into play. See chapter 5.)

In the behavioral space, we were fighting against many digital marketing groups that were not *treatment* centers but rather *call* centers. They were in the

INTELLIGENCE

business of selling leads. Many industries struggle with deceptive online marketing practices.

In 2011 and 2016, *The New York Times* did pieces highlighting how marketing companies had flooded the locksmith space to exploit online advertising and search engine optimization to mislead consumers seeking legitimate locksmith services. These scammers created thousands of pages to mimic legitimate locksmiths and would subcontract the work or sell the leads. This led to higher prices and subpar service.

You must practice situational awareness and know what's happening at all times. Intelligence applies to the platforms on which you build your business. You need to follow and understand what algorithm updates Google is rolling out. You need to understand what new privacy restrictions Facebook is launching. You need to know what new offerings are available on YouTube. Trust that your competitors know and that they will be responding and taking advantage.

There are many examples of allied countries switching sides in war. Italy switched sides to the Allied powers in 1943, further destabilizing Nazi control of Europe. In 1812, Sweden famously switched from supporting Napoleon to joining the Sixth Coalition led by the United Kingdom, Russia, Prussia, and Austria. Sweden's contribution of troops helped secure Napoleon's defeat at the Battle of Leipzig a year later.

You have to stay informed of changing landscapes or risk being exiled, as Napoleon was.

Understand Your Company and Your Team's Strengths

Hannibal understood that he had some weaker troops. He put them at the center of his plan to help with his whole strategy. It takes a lot for a general to say, "I've got some troops that aren't well-trained. That's probably on me. How can they help me in this battle? I will position them here and then put my stronger troops on the wings and the cavalry on the flat."

It works the same for CMOs.

You're going to have some companies that are good at videos. Some companies are good at social. You'll know your team's strengths and weaknesses, and there's no use trying to fake that you're strong everywhere. You need to honestly assess where your strengths are and then figure out how to exploit them.

Gather Intelligence to Create Impact

Almost every company I have worked with as a consultant has had legacy issues or inherited organizational dysfunction. I think, at some level, when a CEO or founder calls me, they suspect this and are looking for confirmation and a road map out of their quagmire.

Gathering intelligence means *you* gather intelligence. If you want to know how the war is going, visit

INTELLIGENCE

the front lines, interview as many staff as possible, hold town halls, talk to vendors and suppliers, and speak to former team members, even if they have left your company. You don't have a lot of time, so quick action to gather intelligence will signal to leadership that they have hired the right person.

**Le moral est au physique comme trois est à un.
(Morale is three times as important.)**
—Napoleon Bonaparte[59]

It's dangerous on the front lines. Napoleon was injured several times during his military campaigns. At the Battle of Ratisbon in 1809, he was shot by a musket ball in his foot while directing troops at the front line. His resilience inspired his soldiers. Luckily you won't be shot leading your team in business, but if your team sees you on the front line, taking calls, taking questions, talking to customers, and responding to complaints, you are more likely to gain their confidence and improve morale.

At Perot Systems, we called this *management by walking around*. You can't lead effectively while sitting behind spreadsheets on your laptop all day in your office.

Addressing the legacy issues is key. Legacy issues go beyond your team; they will live in your partners and suppliers. When I start a consulting engagement, I am always surprised by how often regular meetings with my client have fallen by the wayside. The constant refrain I hear is, "We used to meet regularly before COVID" or "We send weekly updates."

To make an impact, you will need all hands on deck, so engage every partner and supplier to help you in your business mission.

Objectivity Is Tied to Revenue

You need to know where the battle is won and lost. Many people in marketing are confused, which represents an advantage for you.

The battle often isn't even on their radar because no one put it on their radar.

Understand that if you're in marketing, you've always got to be tied to revenue. If you are tied to revenue, you're going to get the raises, the bonuses, and the growth of your team because your goals match the business goals, growth, and revenue. If you're not tied in or there's some break and people are not sure how your work impacts the business, you won't get anywhere.

That's what I love about the whole Hannibal lesson. I think about that morning when all the Romans arrived with their flags and trumpeters, and everything would have looked so beautiful.

INTELLIGENCE

They looked the part, but they weren't tied to the revenue.

───── ★ ─────

If you are marketing from a fairly static annual budget, you're viewing marketing as an expense. Good marketers realize that it is an investment.
—Seth Godin[60]

───── ★ ─────

Some CEOs and CFOs will consider marketing a "tax" and want to pay as little as possible. If you are interviewing for a position at a company with that mentality, run. The lack of strategic investment will be evident in the company's marketing approach, but it will also appear as a lack of capital investments, disrespect for human capital investments, and aging products and services. No one will give you anything; you have to adopt their mental model. Intelligence will feed you the data to make an impact that matches the expected growth and revenue.

I've helped numerous marketing leaders transform their "branding" spending into ROI. You cannot tell most CFOs that there is no ROI because it is a branding exercise. If that thought is in your head, you will have a tough time growing your business and reputation. You have to translate the dollars you spend into measurable results. It requires you to create new metrics to add to your plan or expand your impact on the business. We talked about being transformational versus transactional. Tie your transformational approach to revenue, and accounting will embrace you.

You have been to the front lines. You have the intelligence. Tie it to revenue, and then you're ready to charge into battle.

INTELLIGENCE

WHAT NEXT?

Apply this with your team.
Assign competitors to study and analyze. Consider this reconnaissance and surveillance. Get the team excited. Have team members prepare a presentation on each assigned competitor's marketing efforts. This also serves as an opportunity for junior leaders to shine and practice their research and presentation skills.

Apply this with your C-suite.
Include appropriate analysis and deliver the intelligence. Tell them this is what we are seeing, and this is how we will use that information to win in our marketing.

Gain a quick win.
During the competitor analysis presentations, find one element that your team can execute that week. This will help get the ball rolling and demonstrate that these presentations are not time wasters but are truly action-oriented.

Chapter 8

COUNTERINSURGENCY

I had an interesting career in the United States Army Reserves. I enlisted at nineteen as a 76Y supply clerk for the 489th Civil Affairs (CA) Battalion in Knoxville, Tennessee. I later went through Officer Candidate School (OCS) and was reassigned back to the 489th as a second lieutenant.

Civil Affairs is a niche and specialized branch of the army that fit well with my studies and interest in political science. When I graduated from OCS through the Tennessee National Guard, there was no basic officer course for the CA branch. I was slotted to attend Armor School in Fort Knox, Kentucky. One of the tasks of a CA unit is to assist in winning the hearts and minds of the civil population by providing *counterinsurgency* options to the commanders.

---- ★ ----

Arguably, the decisive battle is for the people's minds.
—*Gen. David Petraeus*[61]

---- ★ ----

The concept of modern counterinsurgency dates back to the American Revolutionary War. During that time, large areas of the colonies supported the British monarch's rule over North America. Gen. George Washington understood the importance of establishing good governance in the areas that patriots were capturing and controlling. Maintaining civil order was key to winning local support.

One notable example of George Washington employing civil affairs during the Revolution was the temporary civil administration he set up in Boston,

COUNTERINSURGENCY

which had been under British control in the early days of the war. Washington's forces laid siege to the city for several months, and by March 1776, the British were forced to evacuate as Washington was able to place cannons above the city on Dorchester Heights.

There was the potential for chaos as the British departed, and Washington shifted his forces into the city to restore order and maintain public safety. He issued orders to his forces that prevented retribution and the confiscation of property owned by Loyalists, which avoided deepening divisions that already existed among the populace and improved the reputation of the Patriots. It was easier to govern by prioritizing the welfare of Boston's citizens.

Washington's actions in Boston were early examples of civil affairs operations, emphasizing the need for governance, protection of civilians, and the promotion of stability in contested areas—principles that remain foundational to modern civil affairs practices in the US Army.[62]

The US Army Civil Affairs and Psychological Operations Command (USACAPOC) was established in 1985 and oversees most civil affairs forces, primarily in the Army Reserve. Today CA supports disaster relief, advises allied forces on governance, and provides expertise in civil-military operations to combatant commanders.

> **In counterinsurgency operations, the decisive effort is rarely military.**
> —*U.S. Government Counterinsurgency Guide*[63]

When Integrating Civil Affairs and Counterinsurgency Goes Wrong

During the 2003 invasion of Iraq, numerous cultural and historical sites were looted and damaged, such as the National Museum of Iraq. Despite warnings from archaeologists and cultural experts, US forces didn't adequately protect them. The loss of cultural artifacts not only devastated Iraq's heritage but also fueled anti-coalition sentiment among the local population. Despite CA units' preparation of cultural asset maps and their readiness to coordinate with local experts and officials, cultural awareness training and coordination with military planners were not fully integrated and realized in the lead-up to the war.

At the same time, hundreds of thousands of former Iraqi military, security, and intelligence soldiers became key players in the insurgency, which led to widespread instability immediately after the invasion. The coalition implemented a sweeping policy called CPA Order Number 2 that disbanded the Iraqi armed services but did not lay out a clear path to reintegrate its members into society. The lack of planning, working with local

COUNTERINSURGENCY

tribal and religious leaders, and employment programs fueled the rise of extremist groups and prolonged the war not just in Iraq but throughout the region.

In the 1992 US presidential election, Ross Perot received nineteen million votes, 19 percent of the popular vote that year. This was the highest percentage for a non-major-party candidate since Theodore Roosevelt's 1912 campaign. We quickly pivoted that force into United We Stand America (UWSA), a citizen action group. In the first year, two million people joined the group, which featured chapters in all fifty states.

After graduating from the University of Tennessee, I became UWSA's national college director. My team helped train our youth supporters on how to get organized and active on their college campuses. UWSA was moving quickly that first year. Besides increasing its activity on campuses, UWSA was working on several fronts:

- Publishing a monthly magazine-style newsletter
- Hosting a national radio program on Sunday nights with Ross Perot
- Experimenting with a version of an electronic town hall pioneered by Dr. Billy Koen at the University of Texas
- Hosting dozens of leaders and politicians at our national convention in 1994, which was broadcast nationally

- Coordinating lots of local meetings in counties and towns across all fifty states

However, when membership was up for renewal a year later, we suffered a major decline. We didn't have good intelligence about what our voters wanted and missed out on the counterinsurgency planning.

We were working hard, but had we inadvertently fallen into looking busy?

I have often had this conversation in my consulting around alumni programs for behavioral health clients. Setting up alumni programs is very important, but be careful. You may feel you are doing some great work setting up more meetings and sending out email newsletters, but is that what the graduates of your program and their families want?

Thinking back to my early years at Foundations Recovery Network, I remember our chief financial officer frequently asking why marketing spend was not decreasing. He wanted to see a reduction in our customer acquisition costs and commented, "I think you're fishing in the wrong ponds." This came from a finance guy who knew little about marketing, and part of his bonus was tied to reducing costs. The lack of intent to learn and understand could have hurt us at a pivotal growth point in our company.

You will hear these types of comments in your career. Sometimes, they are well-intentioned, and other times,

COUNTERINSURGENCY

they are purposely derisive. This situation is known as the Dunning-Kruger effect, a cognitive bias in which people with less ability and knowledge in an area overestimate their competence. This effect often leads people to make statements or give advice that appears overly simplistic to those with more experience. The Dunning-Kruger effect essentially boils down to a lack of awareness of one's limitations in a particular area.[64]

---★---

Ignorance more frequently begets confidence than does knowledge.
—Charles Darwin[65]

---★---

When I heard his fishing comment, I thought, *We're not selling widgets.* With fishing, you put a worm on the

hook, drop it in, and catch a bite. You reel it in, gut it, clean it, and then eat it.

But we worked in health care. Our intention was to help patients solve their medical problems and release them back into society. If you did a good job, they'd refer you to more people.

I had to explain to our finance team that the goal of Foundations was to be *transformational*, not *transactional*. Yes, we might have been spending $3,000 on pay-per-click advertising to attract a new customer, but we also had to factor in the lifetime value of that customer, who, if we did it right, would refer us to other patients.

In contrast, fishing, to borrow the CFO's analogy, is a one-and-done transaction. There is no lifetime value there. You never hear from that fish again—because you ate it.

The CFO's singular focus on going after the lower acquisition cost was rooted in other factors. Perhaps cash was low, insurance reimbursements were late, capital outlays had increased, or maybe he had just looked at his bonus plan. His assumption was flawed; from his perspective, all marketing is created equal, and all channels make a similar contribution at similar costs and volume. So, he thought, *If paid search is more expensive, let's shift budget to the cheaper channels.*

Remember the anvil-and-hammer chapter? You cannot have all hammers! This attitude will lead a company to miss the opportunity to build leverage and scale. The idea of marketing presenting an à la carte menu of options to be selected by another department or committee will place you in an untenable situation.

---— ★ ———

You can't cut your way to prosperity.
—Jeff Skillen[66]

———— ★ ———

The fishing analogy was unfortunate and demonstrated this CFO's lack of awareness. This was classic oversimplification; we were not selling a transactional relationship.

In a transactional relationship, the customer knows what they want to buy: the five-dollar item. *Here's my money; give me the product.* There's no relationship necessarily established with the seller.

Services that depend on some aspect of human interaction are relational. Education services like private schools, tutoring, test preparation, or flight schools are won through the relationship. Health care such as behavioral health rehabilitation services, dental, optometry, plastic surgery, and weight loss all have a relationship marketing component.

Transformation is at the core of successful relationship marketing. Your service is judged on the transformation. Things like price and location become secondary to the transformational impact your services have on customers' life and well-being.

What's Wrong with a Transactional Relationship?

In my career, I have listened to more than ten thousand incoming phone calls for help. This started early at Foundations Recovery Network as we got our phone system straightened out. As our business grew, so did our admissions center. Early on, the call center was based out of our Memphis residential treatment center but was moved to Nashville so we could service all our locations more independently.

This centralized process of answering phone calls was new to the behavioral health industry. Most individual treatment centers answered their calls. This inadvertently contributed to a transactional approach to each call. The call went nowhere if the center answering was not a perfect fit. As I started listening to phone calls, it became evident that we approached customers like we were standing at a drive-through window. A patient or loved one would call, and we would present our services and price and move on. We were missing the life-changing effect our services had on individuals and families. By focusing on technical elements like price and location, we were missing the transformational elements of our treatment services, such as recovery rates, alumni programs, and innovative treatment modalities.

COUNTERINSURGENCY

In the relational services I mentioned previously, the financial model you apply will be stunted if you don't elicit the lifetime value. Your marketing spend will not be an investment; it will just be consumption, one and done.

In behavioral health, a transactional relationship looks like this: The customer calls, gives their insurance details, pays their deductible or copay, gets admitted, goes to the treatment center for the appropriate length of stay, and then goes home. A behavioral health call or admissions center that approaches patients transactionally doesn't see as many admissions. The transactional call center is focused on processing as many calls as possible and verifying benefits as quickly as possible without connecting the caller to the unique elements of the treatment they could receive at their center.

Every patient remembers the place where they got sober. We, the recovery center, became a part of that person's life forever. Many of those patients want to give back. If they had a transformational experience, they want to stay in touch with us forever. They become lifelong advocates, helping point other people in our direction to transform their lives too. The admissions center that approaches each call from the transformational perspective will get referrals from people who were not even admitted to their center.

The lifetime value of this customer has increased exponentially.

In the transactional relationship, yes, the person found sobriety, but they just left, and there's no more relationship. They're not connected to your alumni, to your research, or by referring friends or family members.

That's exactly what I witnessed at one of our failing rehab centers that was more focused on transactions than transformations.

La Paloma, our Memphis treatment center, was underperforming on expected admissions and length-of-stay metrics. Our global CEO, Rob Waggener, and the regional group CEO, Paige Bottom, asked me to conduct a deep-dive analysis and find solutions.

They were receiving negative reviews related to their location. We'd heard from referral sources that they feared sending patients because the area had become a little run-down. The feedback included, "La Paloma is just not going to work for our referrals due to the condition of the residence" and "The consensus among several other guests is that the residence was in poor shape."

I was surprised to learn that the center was on a large plot of urban landscape, twelve acres in the city. With that kind of acreage, it seemed it could have been positioned as a safe oasis in this big urban area, but it wasn't.

We arrived and discovered a dilapidated property. The staff disagreed with our impression of its state. It was a classic example of *creeping normality*, best demonstrated by the metaphor of the boiling frog effect. Significant negative changes had accumulated over several months and years. The staff adapted to the overall declines, which then became normalized. In short, the staff there simply could not see the property through the untainted eyes of visitors.

When our Nashville team toured the facility, we noticed an odd guardhouse with no one there, and the entry gate had a broken arm. The flagpole in the center of the lawn flew an American flag that was faded, torn, and tattered. The lawn sprinklers had stopped working, and what was once a green lawn was strewn with patchy, struggling grass and dusty sections of dirt.

We heard stories from the staff that people would drive in, park in the visitor spots, and then look at the areas surrounding the front door. They would then back out of the parking spot without getting out of the car, do a U-turn, and leave.

Foundations Recovery Network was originally a small mom-and-pop company until it received an investment from a Chicago private equity firm. One of the first centers they bought was La Paloma. Built in the 1920s by the Firestone Foundation as a children's rehabilitation hospital, La Paloma was originally called Children's Rehabilitation Services when Foundations acquired it. That had closed down during World War II, and the building had been used for different kinds of rehabilitation since then.

After the acquisition, Foundations asked themselves, "What are we going to call this place?"

"Well, it's near a residential neighborhood street called La Paloma Street. Let's call it La Paloma."

The patients and local community had no affinity or connection with the name. The street was named La Paloma Street, but it was a Latin-inspired name that seemed to have no tie to Memphis. La Paloma could be a fine name in other parts of the United States, but in Memphis the connection had either never been made or was lost.

During our consultation period with all stakeholders, the CFO stated that he thought we should be getting more referrals from outside the local area. He didn't understand why we couldn't become a national center, flying people in from California. Some people thought we should be solely local, while others thought we should be regional.

So, I ran a study of all the admissions. We were relying on local patients who had some of the lowest reimbursements rates. Our referrals from other centers and interventionists, usually not restricted to insurance, had deteriorated. What was driving the decrease in referrals? We attributed that to the poor state of the facility and the slow decline of our reputation.

If you were local, it was becoming known as a place of last resort, not the first choice. Maybe that also affected contracted insurance rates. So, why start a regional or national marketing effort? That would have been transactional. We would have spent money only to watch people arrive and make an immediate U-turn out of there.

We saw no chance of La Paloma becoming a nationally recognized center in its current state. The analysis we were doing in Memphis also impacted other business and operational aspects of the facility. We saw a chance to improve staff recruiting, increase organizational commitment from team members, and create higher employee retention due to better job satisfaction.

Creeping normality had led to La Paloma approaching the relationship with patients as transactional, not transformational. From a transactional perspective, a patient would only ever stay for thirty days and then graduate, never to be heard from again. Why spend more gaining a client than you have to?

If we were going to turn the center around, we needed to take a transformational approach.

We wanted to establish a relationship with the patient because that connection would encourage the patient to join our alumni program and collaborate with us on customer research. If they had a great experience, they would refer people back to us, which would lower our lifetime cost of acquisition.

Following our presentation, analysis, and recommendations, the executive team agreed to give the property a $1 million facelift.

As we spent time at the property, we looked for ways to connect the facility to Memphis. Memphis is so well known for music. Everyone remembers Elvis, B. B. King, Jerry Lee Lewis, and Carl Perkins from earlier generations, but it is also relevant today with artists like Three 6 Mafia, Yo Gotti, Justin Timberlake, and Valerie June. We knew music (and the arts in general) could better tie our center to Memphis.

Jeff Skillen, a communications consultant we had on retainer for many years, immediately started educating our team on the Memphis music scene. His knowledge led us to design our space after the famous Ardent Studios, founded in 1967 by John Fry. Led Zeppelin, Isaac Hayes, ZZ Top, R.E.M., and the White Stripes had all taken advantage of the high-quality acoustics that Ardent offered. Jeff pitched the idea of The Blue Door recording studio. We discovered that one of the therapists at La Paloma used music in individual and group sessions to help patients process their trauma and addiction, and they were champing at the bit to get involved.

We were suddenly repurposing a room as a studio and painting the door blue. David Perez, the facility CEO, found the perfect space, and he realized we were solving a few problems (force multiplication). This was not only critical in appealing to patients but also changed the human resources factor. We were making La Paloma a patient's first choice and a place where people wanted to work and stay.

COUNTERINSURGENCY

When we opened the recording studio, people chose to come because they were in active addiction, but they also had some connection to music in their past. They used to either play or write music. The studio's tagline, "Find Your Song Within," meant so much to people looking for help because it signaled an ability to reconnect to their lives before addiction.

Art became another key element at La Paloma. They developed a wonderful art therapy program, and their alumni coordinator, Carol Ricossa, had a beautiful way of showcasing art from patients and alumni around the facility. The heart was there, the program was there, but we were missing a way to connect it to the center's story.

The Foundations corporate office was located in Nashville, where I and most of my team worked. Nashville is home to more than a hundred murals spread across various neighborhoods. These photo-friendly works showcase the artistic fabric that makes Nashville a center of creativity. Back at La Paloma we found a two-story brick wall in the rear of the patient housing building that was perfect. It was a long-neglected area that bordered some of the natural twelve-acre campus but was also near the dumpsters and employee parking. We turned this area into a welcoming environment, making it a space that would no longer be cut off from tours and would warmly greet staff each morning as they arrived to work. This mural signaled to everyone that we were serious about using art to reconnect patients to a life of long-term recovery.

Plus, the mural wasn't even that expensive. It cost just a few thousand dollars, right in line with what we spent fixing the tattered flag, broken entry gate, and some sprinkler heads. Many times, it's the ten-dollar fixes that can have big impacts.

These small things, on their own, may not seem like much. But when you put them together, you create transformational change. That's why you must protect each part of your comprehensive plan. You can't have an overall marketing plan and then let somebody start removing bits and pieces to save money.

The mural itself will not bring in more patients, but it is a key part of the transformational system. The system doesn't function without it.

I explained to the finance team that I wanted to be responsible for the spending and have it in our marketing, but just because we were doing a mural didn't mean the mural would lead directly to one admittance. Rather, it would play a role in *every* admission. We envisioned it being in the stories that business development would share with professional referral sources. It would be viewed on every tour, present in multiple articles on the website for SEO purposes, shared across social media channels, and featured in the backdrop of selfies that families take and share about their loved one's successful journey to sobriety.

Suddenly, we had a property that people were proud to showcase when they toured it. The business development team was proud to show it off, and the alumni team was proud to identify with it. It became easier to attract and keep staff.

After our Memphis turnaround, the other group and facility CEOs asked our team to do the same for them. Before long, we had to create a schedule for Malibu, Michigan, and Atlanta. The work led to similar efforts at companies I worked for and consulted with after my Foundations days.

It significantly impacted the bottom line and the morale of the business at a pivotal moment. We were in the early stages of talking with UHS, which a few months later would consummate their acquisition of Foundations for what was, at the time, one of the largest deals in behavioral health care.

That turnaround in Memphis was made possible only because we won the hearts and minds of the staff, professional referral sources, and alumni.

WHAT NEXT?

 Apply this with your team.
Identify the services or products you could frame as transformational in your customers' lifestyle. Something that you have approached transactionally but could have the opportunity to build into a transformational relationship that would keep them engaged with your future offerings or products.

 Apply this with your C-suite.
Apply the math for a lifetime and factor transformational relationship into your budget. Embrace the return on investment and create your metrics.

 Gain a quick win.
Target the group that purchased a product or service, soliciting them for reviews or a new purchase. Don't let perfect be the enemy of good here. Celebrate even a handful as you build your best practices. Rome wasn't built in a day. The key is that you are building and communicating the continued growth.

Chapter 9

WORKING WITH ALLIES

We readily recognize the importance of going into battle with allies, but have you ever been asked who your allies are in business or marketing?

During the Hundred Years' War, King Henry V's invasion of France slowed due to disease and exhaustion after his capture of the French port of Harfleur. King Henry attempted an organized retreat to the English-held town of Calais when the French forces near Agincourt engaged his vastly outnumbered army.

Estimates put the size of the English force at around six thousand and the French force between twenty and thirty thousand soldiers. But King Henry possessed a secret weapon on the battlefield that day—his Welsh longbowmen.

Wales is one of the four countries that make up the modern United Kingdom, alongside England, Scotland,

and Northern Ireland. Located on the western part of the island of Great Britain, Wales has a distinct cultural and historical identity characterized by its language, traditions, and heritage.

Wales had been conquered by Edward I in 1283, and numerous rebellions had ensued in the intervening years. Despite this history, King Henry fostered cooperation with the Welsh. While firmly under English political control, Henry allied with the population and incorporated them into his military campaigns.

The Welsh longbowmen, a relatively small but elite group within Henry V's army, proved to be the decisive factor in the Battle of Agincourt in 1415.

The Welsh were equipped and trained with the very capable armor-piercing longbow. Their longbow was designed to be more than six feet tall and made from yew wood. The arrows could travel two hundred yards, and the Welsh archers could shoot ten to twelve arrows per minute, which was more rapid than crossbows and the early gunpowder weapons of the time. The bow was deeply ingrained in Welsh life, and they were trained from a young age to use it for hunting.

This expertise allowed them to engage the French forces from a great distance.

Henry's forces built walls of protective stakes and positioned the Welsh archers behind them. The Welsh archers could launch barrages of arrows, disrupting the French attacking formations. Chaos ensued among the French lines, and this disruption allowed the smaller English force to counterattack decisively.

This small contingent of allied longbowmen dramatically affected the successful outcome for the English.[67]

You Need Specialist Allies in Your Marketing

At Foundations Recovery Network, a small but consistent source of patients entering our programs came via individual *interventionists*. You may be familiar with the role of interventionists in movies or television shows. Families work with certified interventionists to determine treatment options for a loved one and then facilitate a family meeting led by the interventionist to educate and convince the loved one to enter treatment and therapy voluntarily.

We viewed these interventionists as allies, but initially we had little to offer them other than the occasional referral from someone who called us struggling to deal with a difficult family member. They were great information ambassadors in our industry. If their clients had a good experience, they eagerly shared, and vice versa.

I approached a few well-known interventionists we regularly dealt with about using our team to assist their marketing efforts. These interventionists were small businesses without marketing departments. They knew how to work with families to get someone into treatment but lacked marketing expertise. The idea was to use our expertise in designing and building websites and video capabilities to showcase these interventionists. We deepened our relationship with these allies by offering support in marketing areas where they struggled but we excelled. In the end, we would get some direct phone calls that we could process and triage, and they would get direct phone calls they would handle and consult on.

Within a few months, we had developed the content and recorded videos of our allies. Well-known interventionists like John Southworth and Ken Seeley, who regularly appeared on TV, were among the first to contribute. Later, Brian O'Shea, Ben Randolph, Judy Sperling, and Joe Cappella recorded videos we professionally produced for them, giving them assets for their use while also helping us build the site.

Our initiative contrasted with the typical marketing approach to partnerships. We focused on giving our allies our best video and web design efforts. It was not an afterthought; we wanted them as impressed with our marketing efforts on their behalf as they were with our treatment approaches for their clients. A true ally wants to see their partner experience the same success that they enjoy.

You have groups or individuals in your business circle who, if you considered them allies, could open up a whole new world of marketing possibilities.

★

The greatest change in corporate culture, and the way business is being conducted, may be the accelerating growth of relationships based not on ownership but on partnership.
—Peter Drucker[68]

★

Another perspective on the concept of allies in your marketing will be services or platforms that may not have a direct referral relationship to your business—like interventionists were to Foundations—but are important to your business's daily operations. Activating these supporting networks can give you a tremendous advantage by expanding your reach and depth.

These types of alliances are also historically important from a military strategy perspective. During the Napoleonic Wars, Britain maintained an alliance with Portugal that had begun several centuries before and was one of the oldest alliances in existence at the time.

Portugal was geographically small, and its military capability was weak compared to that of its neighbors, Spain and France. However, this nation was critical in the Duke of Wellington's efforts to defeat French expansion on the Iberian Peninsula. Portugal allowed the British to harbor along its coastline, and the Portuguese army was reorganized under British advice and underwent training by the British. Local Portuguese militias were armed by the British and encouraged to disrupt French supply lines. The British made effective use of what Portugal had to offer.[69]

A great example of business alliances that mutually promote marketing objectives is the collaboration between Red Bull and GoPro.

Red Bull created an entire market segment with its energy drink development in the 1980s. The drink targets athletes, gamers, and young, energetic people looking for a quick performance boost.

GoPro was founded in 2001 and has become the leader in personal action sports video and photography through its waterproof portable cameras and video devices. It started out targeting surfers and has evolved into the go-to equipment for skateboarders, winter sports enthusiasts, thrill-seeking adventurists, and even car event drivers.

The partnership evolved as Red Bull and GoPro were involved in different ways at similar events. The Red Bull Rampage, a mountain biking event, always had participants already using GoPros to capture the action, and the GoPro user was often a Red Bull customer. GoPro CEO Nicholas Woodman said of the alliance,

> Red Bull's global scale and execution is something to be admired. This partnership is very strategic for GoPro. We share the same vision . . . to inspire the world to live a bigger life. While we've worked closely for many years, as official partners we'll be able to more effectively help one another execute our shared vision and scale our respective businesses. GoPro and Red Bull, as a match, are as good as it gets.[70]

Isn't an Ally Just a Marketing Partnership?

The distinction between an ally and a marketing partner lies in the depth of commitment, alignment of values, and mutual benefit of the relationship. A marketing partnership will focus on the financial commitment, while an ally shares your values.

In military terms, a marketing partner is like using mercenaries—people who can serve as hired guns for a time but are not fully committed and connected to your success beyond the temporary monetary connection.

An ally relationship is transformational versus transactional. Allies share your commitment to a common cause and vision. They'll often advocate for your success in ways that align with their principles.

The marketing partnership, in contrast, is shorter-lived and will focus on the promotional qualities of the engagement, not your long-term success.

In addition to cosponsored events, Red Bull and GoPro feature each other in their advertisements and marketing material. They coshare social media campaigns and cocreate them, with both teams working side by side and collaboratively.

The ally will be an advocate and have a deeper personal relationship. Allies share a long-term commitment to their partner's brand, and their relationship is durable in the ups and downs of business cycles. The impact of the ally relationship includes intangible benefits like reputation, credibility, shared innovation, and even societal change, as seen in the Susan G. Komen Foundation or Foundations Recovery Network's Heroes in Recovery campaigns.

Where Do You Find Your Allies?

Finding allies among your greater business partners will require you to be creative in designing marketing opportunities that make sense. At Foundations, we created speaking opportunities for some of our vendors at conferences we hosted. In return, we sought opportunities to appear at their events, on their YouTube channel, or on their podcast platforms. We weren't expecting direct patient referrals from these opportunities, but we were achieving content authority, which helped drive our rankings and led to more patients.

Look for indirect opportunities, but figure out the quantifiable reasons. Your allies could help you with staff recruiting, training, content, vendor relationships, geographies, and so on. You may not see an opportunity at first, so look beyond the obvious referral relationship.

In our personal and professional endeavors, we are quick to recognize the people and supporters who help us achieve our goals—the parents or siblings who've sacrificed for us or that teacher who stayed late to help advise us on a project. If you look among your corporate network, you will find businesses that can provide instrumental support to your goals and celebrate together with you as you achieve them.

WHAT NEXT?

 Apply this with your team.
Your team is a great way to discover allies. Allow them to grow and nurture these relationships, and invite them to present on ally opportunities regularly.

 Apply this with your C-suite.
Your approach to allies in marketing could have additional benefits with members of the C-suite. Perhaps the relationship you've built eventually aids in acquisitions or referrals for new business and product lines. Invite your CEO and CFO to meet their counterparts among your allies.

 Gain a quick win.
Find an ally you can host on your podcast and vice versa. Then, let the cross-promotion flourish among your citizen soldiers and into your marketing.

Chapter 10

CIRCUMVALLATION

The first few months at Foundations Recovery Network were a whirlwind. It was my first opportunity with a "chief" title—chief information officer (followed by chief marketing officer soon after)—and my first exposure to behavioral health care.

At Foundations, I was introduced as the "marketing guy," to which I would say I'm really the "data guy." I let the data guide my marketing decisions. Many of the data points I needed were gathered manually at that time, as there were no integrated dashboards. I made a point of checking marketing data like analytics before leaving my house in the morning, manually logging in to each account to input the data in our marketing data spreadsheet, which I kept on a shared drive. By the time I arrived in the office, I was already up to speed on the trend from the day before.

During those first few weeks, I realized we were not just competing with other behavioral health treatment providers. We also had a second front: the marketers who had set up websites to gather leads to sell to healthcare providers. These savvy Internet marketers leveraged their marketing expertise in organic SEO and paid search to gain rankings on major search engines like Google, Yahoo, and Bing. They sold leads and phone calls to actual providers. It was the same game I discussed in chapter 7, where lead-generating call centers were intercepting the public's online searches for locksmiths in New York City.

As we were researching our center's website rankings, we'd see multiple new websites appearing with generic drug and alcohol keywords in their website and domain name. The websites were keyword-heavy, with lots of eye-catching stock photography. I would secretly shop on these sites, call in, and go through the process like a potential patient. The person answering these calls would have a script and offer to take my information and connect me with a treatment provider. They would then "transfer me" to a place that would immediately request my insurance information and start selling me on why I should travel to their facility for treatment.

It was the Wild West. The lead-generation aggregators started proliferating. A patient or loved one would see a website and think they were calling a center, but it was a directory that would then sell your inquiry to an actual treatment provider based on who would pay the most for that lead. It was a deceptive tactic that the unethical yet savvy digital marketers had perfected in the insurance, legal, and locksmith industries. And it wasn't just fooling web visitors; it was happening in Yellow Pages listings, billboards, and television ads.

We were really not competing with providers such as the Caron Foundation, Betty Ford, Cumberland Heights, Promises, Alina Lodge, and Sierra Tucson. These traditional and well-known behavioral health treatment centers were facing similar challenges. As the author Spencer Johnson would say, "Their cheese had been moved."[71]

Were we powerless in this new online search dynamic?

We couldn't wait for intervention from the Federal Trade Commission or an investigation by a committee in Congress for relief. (The US Congress finally opened an investigation nine years later.) Google lacked the incentive to correct the problem that was now contributing to the growing addiction crisis. The search engine's auction marketplaces were now surging with new ads from these new lead-generation sites. These lead peddlers were now profiting by selling leads from a vulnerable population to low-quality, low-efficiency insurance-draining locations that then dumped these unsuspecting patients without treating their underlying condition or rehabilitating them appropriately. It was a vicious cycle that was further fueling the opioid crisis affecting America.

Growing up the son of a military history buff, I was always encouraged to read the history books my father kept on his shelf. I would regularly reread parts of Julius Caesar's commentaries.[72] Why was Caesar coming to mind for me during this time, specifically, his circumvallation?

The Battle of Alesia

The Battle of Alesia may best illustrate Caesar's military genius. Located in the eastern part of modern-day France, Alesia consisted of a fortress built on top of Mont Auxois.

The conquest of Alesia was part of Caesar's campaign to conquer and pacify Gaul during the Gallic Wars. Caesar needed this win to send a message to the other tribes in what is now present-day France: Resisting Rome's power was futile.

Caesar besieged this strong hilltop fort because a direct attack on the Gallic forces would have been useless. The Gauls, led by Vercingetorix, were well entrenched, and the direct attack uphill would have cost Caesar's legion numerous casualties. He knew the fort's food supply wouldn't last long with eighty thousand inhabitants, so he built walls around the mountaintop fortress.

CIRCUMVALLATION

Caesar also knew, though, from his network of allies, spies, and captured enemy soldiers, that a large Gallic army was being gathered to attack him and relieve Alesia. So, he built a second set of walls to protect his forces from potential reinforcements. This technique is called *circumvallation*—a fort around a fort.

The siege constructed at Alesia was not uniform in layout. Time and labor were saved by building shorter walls, thinner breastworks, and shallower ditches in some areas, such as on the higher ground, that could be more easily defended.

Ditches were dug with five rows of stakes made from tree trunks. The tips were sharpened, and the trunks, left with their branches in place, created green, leafy pits that impaled anyone trying to traverse them. The Roman soldiers referred to this area of defense as the gravestones.

Beyond were the lilies—stakes smoothed and sharpened at the tip, buried with only a foot extruding from the ground and covered with leaves, moss, and twigs, creating a painful discovery for the Gauls.

Finally lay the spurs—a harrowing discovery to aggressors who ventured over them. They were logs laid in rows with sharp iron hooks protruding from them. Any delay in crossing these defenses allowed the Romans to easily pick them off with arrows and spears.

---•---

On reconnoitering the situation of the city, finding that the enemy were panic stricken, because the cavalry in which they placed their chief reliance, were beaten, he encouraged his men to endure the toil, and began to draw a line of circumvallation round Alesia.
—*Julius Caesar*[73]

---•---

Examples of this circumvallation technique date back to the Greeks and their encirclement of Syracuse in the Peloponnesian War.

During the Middle Ages, circumvallation became more sophisticated as advancements in military technology allowed for the construction of more elaborate fortifications. Moats, drawbridges, and towers became common, and circumvallation was employed in numerous sieges, such as the Siege of Constantinople in 1453.[74]

In the early modern period, circumvallation continued, particularly during the Thirty Years' War (1618–48), when Protestant and Catholic armies employed the practice extensively. The famous Siege of Vienna in 1683 also featured a circumvallation of the city by the Ottoman army.[75]

With the advent of modern warfare in the nineteenth and twentieth centuries, circumvallation became less common, as it was no longer an effective strategy against modern armies' increasingly powerful weapons and tactics. However, it still remains an integral part of military history and strategy, and the term is still used in modern military discourse.

I Needed to Engage Our True Competitors

Returning to my challenge at Foundations, I had an interesting dilemma. I needed to engage our real competitors—not the lead-generating call centers but rather the other health-care companies who provided rehab services similar to our offerings. But these well-funded interlopers were also attacking us and siphoning leads by attacking our position in search engines.

We were busy rebuilding and designing our main corporate website and facility-specific websites, which were focused on competing with our true competitors. In my mind, we were laying effective siege to our competition, and it was only a matter of time before our strategy started to win out. However, we now had these digital marketing companies building websites and advertising in paid search to attract visitors and then sell the leads. We had to build a fort around a fort.

I literally drew a circle around a circle on a whiteboard.

There were thousands of keyword combinations and phrases that a patient or loved one could use in searching for help online, and these marketers had figured out that they could spin up dozens of websites

quickly without worrying about the key components of conversion on our facility sites that we worried about.

Their sites didn't have staff bios, high-quality facility photos, virtual tours, and the like. They were counting on consumer behavior, which involved clicking on only the very top results. As mobile started to dominate, these consumers just clicked and called with very little time spent on the page.

I used the idea of circumvallation to educate and sell our new strategy internally. We would launch dozens of sites targeting very specific keyword sets and phrases. These sites would be optimized only for those small sets of keywords, lightweight and speedy, and include keywords in the domain. We went from five websites to more than a hundred websites in time.

You would not necessarily build a hundred websites today to win in search, but the key takeaway here is that you have to be strategic. Sometimes, applying a military strategy component can help you win the day in the C-suite or the boardroom. The fort around a fort concept helped explain a sometimes-difficult marketing plan. Everyone understands that reinforcements may arrive when laying siege. Everyone also understands that having excellent engineering makes sense. Moving the status quo required more than just explaining the details; executives needed to grasp the historical parallel. All of a sudden, the marketing black hole was illuminated.

Today's "Own the First Page" Strategy

Circumvallation lives on today in the modern "own the first page" marketing strategy.

Imagine you're trying to rank number one for "alcohol rehab Tennessee." Someone is ranking higher than you for that term. You create authoritative content to push up the rankings. The competitors are not sitting idly by, letting you take their spot. They are immediately rushing in with reinforcements.

The competitors could put more resources toward video, podcasts, and directory listings. If they lose that first rank based on a blog post or a website post, they'll attack you on other channels quickly to get a foothold and regain lost ground.

You have to plan and budget for the response. Caesar didn't wait for the Gallic reinforcements to arrive; he had the intelligence and knew they were on the way.

You must budget, staff, and schedule to prepare a new fort around your fort. If you win the ranking battle, you don't want to turn around the next day and lose it.

Gen. George Patton once said, "I don't like paying for the same real estate twice."[76] Neither does your finance department nor your investors. They would rather you win and then own the fort for a while.

You're going to create this budget and plan to get your website and this blog post to rank number one, but you've got to also cover positions two, three, four, five, six, and seven. Simultaneously, while you're working on the blog post, you've got to work on these other platforms.

You can't just put all your eggs in the keyword copy basket. What are you doing on video? What are you doing on podcasts? What are you doing on directory listings? What are you doing on social media? Those are just as important to defend as what you're trying to do with that number one position.

Most people think of Yelp as a place to search for restaurant reviews, but because Yelp is so dominant in restaurants, it shows up for all sorts of search terms. You can even search for your local Target or Walmart, and Yelp will be on the first page.

Similarly, treatment centers in the United States have got to have a really good Yelp page. Even though people aren't necessarily going to Yelp to find you, Yelp often shows up somewhere on the first search page.

CIRCUMVALLATION

It takes up one of those page-one positions.

Potentially, so do all of these: podcasts, YouTube, Facebook, Instagram, paid search, directories, photos, Google My Business, crowdsourced listings, news, and PR.

You're going after a specific keyword or phrase in the top position. I get it, but that's only one thing. You've got multiple spots in rankings on that page. We've got to build a fort around the other positions on the page while you target the top positions. Your competitors are all coming after you, and they'll now have nine places or more to try to attack you and move up. Don't give them an easy opening in your wall or let them quickly establish a beachhead to siphon your leads. You are trying to keep them at bay and as far down the page as possible.

------ ★ ------

In preparing for battle I have always found that plans are useless, but planning is indispensable.
—Dwight D. Eisenhower[77]

------ ★ ------

Communicating the Plan

Every great military leader has a deadly weak point—communications. If you cannot communicate the battle plans effectively, you will lose. Creating a plan and being able to communicate it simply and effectively to the entire team is critical.

Caesar experienced that problem at the Battle of Gergovia, which preceded his success at Alesia. The Gallic leader, Vercingetorix, convinced some of his Gallic countrymen who were supporting Caesar to switch sides and join him. Upon learning of the defection, Caesar ordered his remaining loyalist Gauls to lead a surprise attack before losing others to Vercingetorix's side. The problem was that Caesar's own legions had heard reports of deserters, and when this column of loyalist Gallic cavalry arrived to assist the Romans, Caesar's forces, fearing they were deserters, started engaging them. By the time the friendly fire was over, Vercingetorix had the upper hand and continued his attack, and Caesar was forced to issue an orderly retreat. The lack of communication had lost the battle for him on this day.[78]

At times, I've worked with marketing agencies on specific projects. Paid search was an area where I could bring in specific expertise to help. While they would understand all about Google Ads, they were new in behavioral health. If we were not communicating effectively, our spending could easily be drained into what the agency would see as "top-performing" keywords and phrases. Why? Because volume reports made it appear that was where the search traffic was. Our paid search campaigns needed eyeballs from consumers

CIRCUMVALLATION

who were more educated about their condition further down the decision path. Our SEO efforts were set up to handle more of the top-of-funnel consumers who were starting their journey. If the communications were ineffective, our agency would be attacking our internal team's efforts, similar to the Roman legion attacking their Gallic allies by accident.

Our circumvallation practice was resource-intensive but in a different way. For the Romans, circumvallation took expertise. Caesar was a great engineer. We don't think enough about the engineering prowess of our marketing teams.

Keywords such as *rehab* and *treatment* were highly competitive from both the value or cost of the service and the high number of providers locally, regionally, nationally, and virtually. We spent most of our time researching and building campaigns focused on words and phrases around the edges, on the periphery of the highly competitive terms. We created our own circumvallation practice, allowing us to encircle our competitors and lay siege and pick off the more competitive terms when the time and auction price fit our battle plans (i.e., budget).

The intensiveness is on the research: researching the words and phrases used by the consumer, researching the competition and bid amounts, and then confirming the conversion process and the expected costs. We had to spend a lot of time "engineering" before we could move to writing ad copy.

It's similar to the "research" that Caesar did in Alesia. The Romans would interrogate Vercingetorix's captured soldiers, seeking information on troop strength and formations. Caesar also pressed his Gallic allies on the involvement of other tribes to determine the potential for forces that could arrive to relieve the surrounded Gallic chieftain.

I often hear complaints like, "We cannot get the details on what is being searched, so we can only guess what terms are converting." There is a reluctance to employ Caesar's techniques and "interrogate" the data we have. In health care, we have several touchpoints where we speak to the patient or the referent. Adding a question about how they heard about us and, if it's a digital lead, a follow-up question about what search term they used to find us gives valuable insight. Most centers I have consulted or trained always have the same initial reaction: "I don't have time for that."

When I present how valuable this data is and frame it as intelligence, they suddenly become excited about how they can help gather this intelligence. Many cloud phone systems also have options to provide you with keywords detected in the conversation. Combining that data with the "interrogation" intelligence, you now have actionable intelligence to deploy and win.

CIRCUMVALLATION

In health care, another reason to ask, "How did you hear about us?" is to ensure that your center is aligned with the potential professional referral source. If you don't know who referred you, you will not ensure that your center provides the recommended service or level of care.

In the behavioral health space, there are thousands of competitors. At any given moment, we could see competitors offering similar care services: detox, residential, partial hospitalization, intensive outpatient, virtual outpatient, sober living, and telehealth. We would also see geographic competition pop up locally, regionally, and nationally, especially as travel for treatment became a convenient and acceptable solution for behavioral health treatment. We would also see new competitors advertising new payer contracts or financing options.

When I set about building a marketing team, one of the first roles I defined was our developer (i.e., engineer) for our digital marketing team. Most people—consumers and marketers, at least—only look at the UX side of the developer role, but I wanted to ensure we were the best at what lay beneath the design.

When the Romans were building siege towers, they had to make sure they were mobile. Designing an amazing-looking siege tower that could not be moved to the walls of Alesia would do Caesar no good. Similarly, designing a heavy website that does not render quickly will not allow you to rank within search results.

I knew we would not always be the largest or have the biggest budgets, but we would outsmart and better engineer our competitors. Our walls, ramparts, and siege machines would be the best.

You not only have to design your digital marketing products at the highest level to win battles but also must engineer your search engine optimization. Building great SEO was like designing the Roman circumvallation techniques for our teams.

We had to break our desired content ranking into tiers:

- Tier 1: Highly competitive general terms with high search volume that were expensive and budget-draining
- Tier 2: Phrases and specific terms known as long tail terms with lower volume, less competition, and less risk to the budget
- Tier 3: General terms with modifiers/addendums such as geographic, directional, and adjectives that were higher volume but less qualified and cheaper but could negatively impact quality

We used circumvallation to create a strategy where we could, in essence, surround the tier 1 content with our tier 2 and tier 3. As we shored up tier 2 and tier 3, we would attack tier 1 when it was advantageous for

CIRCUMVALLATION

us to do so. We would attack on the weekends or late in the day, look for competitors that exhausted their budgets early in the month, watch for media coverage on any of our terms that could increase volume quickly, and react.

You should never go to battle before you've won the war on paper.
—Philip Kotler[79]

We have all these marketing terms and functions, such as *omnichannel, enterprise, brand positioning, demand generation, lead nurturing, personas, account-based marketing, contextual marketing, WOM, churn, automation, top-of-funnel, retention,* and *expansion*. Our teams can get so focused on their narrow piece that they sometimes forget the battle they are in and how their piece supports the mission. Remind them of their role in the battle.

WHAT NEXT?

 Apply this with your team.
Gather phone, live chat, and form lead data on keywords appearing in conversations from your leads. Analyze and look for what your customers are telling you about how they discover your services.

 Apply this with your C-suite.
Use circumvallation to educate the C-suite leaders about why you have to attack but also defend the territory you are seizing in search. As you build positions, don't abandon them in the weeks or months after you win; maintain them. Draw a circle around a circle on your whiteboard to illustrate the concept.

 Gain a quick win.
Create updated profiles on some of the listing sites where your company should appear. Create the *best* profiles, maintain them, watch them appear in searches, and start moving toward the first page.

Chapter 11

OPERATIONAL READINESS

It felt like we were starting to clean our weapons the moment we stepped off the bus for basic training. The drill sergeants entered the front of the bus and, in a flurry of shouts to "hurry it up," ordered us to deboard the 1970s-era Blue Bird bus. We stumbled off the bus,

rushed to grab our bags from the pile of others thrown on the ground, and then stood in some sort of formation.

A few days later, we received our designer clothing, visited the hair stylist, and were introduced to our weapon and the concept of preventive maintenance checks and services (PMCS).

Next, we began learning to fire our weapons. We shot for ten minutes and then cleaned our guns for the next two hours. We each asked ourselves (and each other), *Why am I cleaning it so much?*

But it wasn't just our weapons. We shined our boots until we could see our reflections. We had to keep the latrine spotless. The barracks were immaculate.

PMCS is a fundamental component of military operational readiness, and experiences in the Vietnam War are a fine example of that.

The US military introduced the M16 rifle to US troops in 1963 as the counterinsurgency operation in Vietnam was escalating into a broader war. The United States military, specifically the army, needed a lightweight alternative to the AR-15, something better suited for jungle warfare. The new M16 was lauded for its lightweight design and firepower, but problems with the weapon arose soon after deployment.

The M16, with its aluminum receiver, steel bolt, barrel, and polymer buttstock, required regular cleaning and lubrication. Despite this, the weapons were sent to the jungle without cleaning kits, and while soldiers

OPERATIONAL READINESS

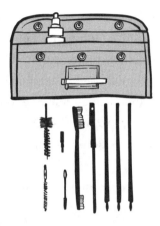

were taught to sight the weapon and fire with accuracy and precision, they were not properly instructed on how to clean and maintain it. This lack of basic maintenance led to excessive carbon buildup inside the rifle's chamber and receiver, which regularly caused jamming, especially in combat.

The weather conditions in the field exacerbated the maintenance requirements. Soldiers experienced hot, wet, and muddy environments, which led to the M16 jamming and misfiring during battle if not kept up with preventive maintenance. Numerous cases were reported of soldiers killed or wounded because their weapons failed.

In the fierce fighting during the Battle of Ia Drang in 1965, many soldiers abandoned their M16s in place of their sidearms or captured Viet Cong rifles during battle.

NEVER OUTMATCHED

The US military sent cleaning kits and conducted rushed training and maintenance schedules as reports piled up. By 1967, a next-generation M16 was launched that included a new chrome-plated chamber to reduce carbon buildup and cleaner-burning ammunition. And once strict adherence to the PMCS schedule for M16s was maintained, the rifle eventually became a trusted weapon.

The consequences of the M16 rollout highlight how easy it is to get focused on the equipment or the technology but lose the battle because of a lack of maintenance or maintenance training. It's true in war ... and it's just as true in your marketing.

Many senior marketers don't formalize something like the military's PMCS structure. That's a big mistake.

In 2006, I had an opportunity to join a digital music start-up in Nashville, Tennessee — "Music City." This was at the beginning of the digital music craze. Napster had launched and was in the subsequent process of being shut down. Our company, PassAlong Networks, had a four-year run as an early innovator in the digital music frontier. We were on the Microsoft platform when Apple had just launched iTunes.

Our six founders, Dave Jaworski, Brad Edmonson, Jozef Nuyens, Scott Lewis, Robin Pou, and Scott Hughes, had created one of the first licensing agreements with the big music labels to take music online legally. Jaworski was a former Microsoft executive,

OPERATIONAL READINESS

Edmonson pioneered digital merchandising for musicians, Nuyens owned a major recording studio in Nashville, Pou was a legal strategist, and Hughes was a music label executive.

Everyone from the founders to the staff brought outside talents to the nascent digital music world. Apple competitors were scrambling to catch up to Steve Jobs, and labels were seeking out alternative platforms. The music labels in Nashville wanted their music wrapped on our platform in the Microsoft digital rights management system. At that time, a flood of MP3 players had hit the market—devices like the Microsoft Zune, the Creative Zen, the iRiver, and the Toshiba Gigabeat—to challenge Apple's iPod. At one point, numerous parties were interested in investing or acquiring us. We were all very excited at the opportunities that laid before us.

These potential opportunities involved many demos and visits to Austin and Seattle, the leading hubs of technology innovation in our space at the time. One particular day, Microsoft executives visited us in Nashville for a tour and demo, as they were rumored to be interested in acquiring our company. That morning, minutes before the Seattle-based executives arrived, one of our music hosting servers failed. Suddenly, numerous executives were now in the IT director's office. Staff were out of their offices and cubes, crisscrossing our space to share the latest information. Someone came into my office and asked me and a coworker to bow our heads in prayer. When staff are resorting to prayer over a server, you know it's bad. It was panic and chaos. Why? Because we had no PMCS.

We were a small digital music start-up working off of fold-up card tables. We'd started with six founders, and by the time I got there, we had forty team members and an initial capital raise north of $40 million within twelve months. We were creating a new business, "ingesting digital music" from the record labels and then "wrapping" those songs in a protective layer, making it instantly available across numerous online stores. The processes and procedures required to support the basic infrastructure were lacking at the time. There were a lot of experimental projects, and we pivoted often to meet customer requests. In all the hustle and bustle, we had neglected some basic maintenance on our server array and were behind on applying patches. Then, on what may have been the most important day in our business's history, we got caught with our pants down.

Like the US military's focus on launching and using new equipment, we were focused on designing and implementing new digital storefronts and database fields, not maintaining them.

So, what happened? Microsoft walked away, we never got a deal in place, and PassAlong Networks faded into the history books of early digital music.

As marketers, it's easy to put simple maintenance tasks on the back burner for what are considered more revenue-important requirements. The reality, though, is that *marketers who fail in the CMO role typically do so because they lack systems*.

PMCS ensures you are judged on marketing and not on a support system failure. The designer of the M16 wanted to be judged positively on the rifle's effectiveness, not poorly because it wasn't maintained properly. In the same way, we wanted PassAlong Networks to be judged for its digital music offering, not for the upkeep of the server the system was running on.

Foundations Recovery Network was the first place I formally introduced PMCS. I remember it clearly because one of the first positions I wanted to hire was a data analyst. Today we have automation tools, which we didn't have back then (everything was checked manually). We needed this analyst to build and monitor monthly reports and dashboards.

Some of my C-suite family didn't understand marketing, so there was pushback, "Why do you need a data analyst? Sounds like unnecessary bureaucracy." The PMCS framework helped me sell them on the idea that if we invest in marketing assets, we need to ensure that investment delivers value. To do that, we need an analyst to help us monitor and maintain those marketing assets. If, for example, we invested $30,000 in a new website, we needed to ensure that we kept adding content to it and that this content performed to its objectives. We had to ensure the integrity of the system we were building to enjoy the yield of a successful outcome.

Why did the PMCS help persuade them? Because it was formalized and provided a clear set of tasks we needed to complete to deliver on our marketing objectives. When I connected results to decisions and decisions to the formal PMCS, this idea of hiring a data analyst didn't sound like marketing hocus pocus anymore.

Kesava "K" Anderson, our new business analyst who had spent a few years at Coca-Cola, was a whiz at Excel. What could have come across as unnecessary bureaucracy and wasteful spending was instead viewed by the C-suite as innovation. K immediately connected with Shawn Manis, Cherie Carter, and me in the marketing team, and soon, we had not only monthly dashboards but also tools that allowed us to show our marketing assets (site traffic, top articles, social activity, etc.), updated in real time and put on a big screen. The real benefit was that all marketing team members now understood their daily impact on our numbers.

Marketing Is a System

One of my big passions is antique cars, especially '70s to early '90s European cars—you know, the types that adorned Gen Xers' dorm room walls and were featured in television shows like *Magnum PI* or *Miami Vice*. One of my favorite cars is my 1993 Lotus

OPERATIONAL READINESS

Esprit. Detractors sometimes jibe that Lotus stands for *Lots of Trouble, Usually Serious*. Meaning, if you don't keep up with the maintenance, it won't start up when you want to get in your car and drive. The vehicle requires regular maintenance, ensuring the proper air pressure is in the tires, the fluids are good, the timing belt is not twenty years old, the battery is charged, and the gas is fresh.

My hobby is showing the few vintage cars I have collected. The idea is to display them as close as possible to how they looked when they came off the production line. To be competitive, everything has to be addressed. I cannot have a fantastic paint job with ripped-up seats. I cannot have windshield wipers that won't move back and forth or a headlight that's burned out. The design and beauty of the car are going to be judged, but the supporting systems are what make that car worthy of a ribbon.

Do you see how all this could be a metaphor for your marketing?

Some departments outside of marketing view what we do as a series of isolated activities, which makes each easier to cut and dismiss. You and I know that's not the case. All individual elements contribute to the performance you're judged by, and to contribute, they must function at all times.

We cannot expect folks outside marketing to understand how the system works. Heck, most people on your team won't understand the complexities of the marketing engine. It's your job to document it, show the team members how to maintain it, and show people outside the team why each component is essential to keep the engine running.

PMCS helps you sell ideas and innovations upstream. Once you formalize every marketing activity and get buy-in for the "operations manual," you eliminate many of the "dumb" questions you often get asked in the boardroom.

We have budget meetings every year. In that meeting, finance will always be tasked with cutting expenses. The PMCS helps you explain how and why each component is critical to the marketing engine (and therefore requires budget). The CFO will ask, "Why do you need this training? Why are we sending somebody to a conference?" If you don't have formalized, documented operations, it becomes easy for somebody who doesn't understand what you do to start picking things off as separate expenses instead of viewing them as an integral part of your comprehensive marketing system.

Without that PMCS, it's easy to get cut down. But with it, you have formal, strategic support for every decision and expense.

PMCS in Action

So, what does a marketing PMCS look like? It consists of the following eight sections.

OPERATIONAL READINESS

1. The Commander's Commitment

When I say *commander*, I mean *leadership team*. It's easy for leaders to cut if they haven't bought into the idea that preventive maintenance is critical to your team's success. It'll be something they suggest skipping or cutting back on when things get busy or budgets tighten. Then, all of a sudden, you go many, many weeks or months where things don't get done.

They'll say, "Let's not renew HubSpot this year. Or you know what? We've got to lay somebody off. Lay off the data analyst." So, before you do anything to build out a PMCS, you need a strategy to get a commander's commitment. If they're not committed, it's worthless.

To be clear, you need the commander's commitment to the PMCS as a whole, not to any particular parts of it. You cannot let other leaders cherry-pick parts to maintain. You're responsible for the marketing PMCS, not other leaders in your organization. Once everybody appreciates that the activities in the PMCS are critical (along with the subsequent maintenance of the PMCS itself as a whole), then everybody falls in line underneath. All your supporting players and employees know they have to do this.

How do you get the commitment? One of the best ways is to secure investment in the PMCS. When the Foundations leadership funded the data analyst position, they categorically decided that it must be important since we're spending hard dollars on this PMCS to support our maintenance schedule. Psychologically and financially, they became invested.

Another example might be a company bringing in software to help track performance and maintenance. That reflects our agreement that this is important. The investment could also be reflected in the time you agree to spend on PMCS. "Hey, we'll spend a week documenting our whole schedule."

In my army days, being made to spend two hours cleaning a weapon I had fired for only ten minutes demonstrated a real investment in PMCS. We could have spent those two hours doing something else, and there was *always* something else we could have been doing. But we were instructed to spend that time maintaining our equipment, and that instruction from the top delivered a message about the importance of PMCS.

2. A Robust Training Program

Now we have the commander's commitment, but if we're going to operate this PMCS, it's got to be robust. It can't be one sentence or checked only once.

A PMCS should be detailed. There should be many weekly tasks, quite a few monthly tasks, and then several annual tasks. You've got to get buy-in from your team, the people conducting the activities in the PMCS. To carry out our correct preventive maintenance, they must understand that the work is thorough and vital.

OPERATIONAL READINESS

These are not box-ticking exercises. We genuinely are doing PMCS.

3. Basic Services

Make sure there's dedicated time for basic services. These are the easy things. Weekly maintenance is generally going to be a basic task. In the digital space, a basic service would be looking at the previous month's blog post and asking,

- How many words were there?
- How many anchor text words did you have?
- How many links did you build back?

These are all things you can easily discern from the numbers.

In the analogy of your vintage car, basic services include putting air in the tires and checking to ensure you've got enough oil.

4. Complex Services

These are usually annual (and/or sometimes monthly) services needed to maintain optimal operation. Sticking with the car example, your annual complex services might involve pulling the engine, which is more complex than the basic services.

With a digital product, a complex service will be a yearly evaluation of the site architecture. That'll take more time than the basic service and it'll often require a more skilled person. I could put a junior person on the weekly task, but someone senior will be responsible for the annual.

5. Eliminate Distractions

When you enter PMCS mode, you're solely focused on PMCS. You're not multitasking. In the military, you're not having someone clean their weapon and do annual marksmanship simultaneously. Those are two competing tasks, and if you're only giving that same amount of time to complete both, they'll shoot and get certified, and then they'll have a shortened window to clean. You're reducing the importance and, subsequently, the results of the PMCS.

Another sign of distraction is postponing a scheduled PMCS task to attend an "important" meeting. No, you need to eliminate distractions.

When I started working at Specialty Care, our CEO, Sam Weinstein, had a great policy during meetings: Don't open cell phones or laptops. It took some getting used to, but what a liberating feeling to be able to listen, engage, and take notes without the distraction of that email or that text. His meetings were shorter, probably because we accomplished more during those times.

6. Quality Control

In section 4, I mentioned putting a junior person on a weekly task. We need to ensure that somebody spot-checks to ensure junior people are doing things correctly. You also need some form of quality control to ensure the data has been checked for accuracy.

In the example of the military, a sergeant's going through the checks. He's not checking that the oil has been changed in all thirty vehicles, but he will spot-check a handful.

My son Cy played high school football at Lipscomb Academy in Nashville as a kicker. I would take many afternoons off to sit quietly in the stands and watch practices. I didn't play football, so I was always interested in learning as much as possible. I enjoyed watching how practices were organized and executed throughout the week.

One of the assistant coaches, Austin Bolen, led the boys in warm-ups and stretches. As will happen with high school boys, the quality of their effort during this portion of the practice was a little suspect. Coach Bolen walked around each line and affirmed, "You are out here, so you might as well do them right!" There will be people on your team from time to time who will think that this is a waste of time or that some other priority should be ahead of this. Remind them of what Coach Bolen would say.

7. Give Them the Right Tools

If you're going to have your team conduct PMCS, are you giving them the right tools? Are you giving them a HubSpot? Are you giving them access to analytics? Do they have a good laptop? They've got to have the proper tools, and when you get buy-in from the very top, it's not an issue when you have to have some of these tools in place to ensure you have a good PMCS strategy.

8. Encourage Proper Performance

This is the marketing of the PMCS. You have to ensure you're letting the team know this is working. They need a feedback loop. If they do all this in a vacuum, they'll slowly drift off and won't take it as seriously.

I saw this all the time in the military, especially when I was at Fort Knox. If we were running maintenance on a tank's tread, or track, the sergeant would occasionally call us over and say, "See, look at this, boys. This track was getting ready to separate and come off the tank." We needed to regularly inspect the tension and clean any debris while looking for worn or damaged track components.

When you see that, think, *Oh, I'm so glad we checked that.* That showed us the value of this PMCS work we were doing.

Sometimes in striving for amazing strategic wins, we forget the routine things that will have a huge impact. Home runs are good, but you better be able to catch that routine pop fly every time.

OPERATIONAL READINESS

WHAT NEXT?

 Apply this with your team.

Create your own PMCS. Keep it basic and straightforward to start. Begin by identifying weekly, monthly, and quarterly activities that you need to do to ensure your company's marketing success. Don't be afraid to document it in Excel or Word, and don't let perfect be the enemy of good.

In marketing, especially digital marketing, you lose if you don't maintain. A well-maintained average plan will beat a fantastic plan that is not maintained every time.

 Apply this with your C-suite.

Include the percentage of completeness to your new PMCS document in your monthly reporting. Let the C-suite know it's important to you, and it will become important to them.

 Gain a quick win.

Showcase a quick win, and if you can display or publish your PMCS, all the better. Celebrate that your team was 100 percent complete on weekly or monthly activities. Eventually, you'll be able to celebrate that these tasks are keeping your SEO, PPC, or social marketing strong.

Chapter 12

COMBAT ORGANIZATION

When I was traveling through the Netherlands a few years ago, we happened upon a historical marker for the Dutch East India Company (*Vereenigde Oostindische Compagnie*, or VOC) in front of a building in Amsterdam. This building was a warehouse, auction house, and headquarters for the VOC, the first corporation in the world to introduce modern corporate practices, such as appointing a board of directors and issuing stock that could be publicly traded. As I was looking around the courtyard and listening to tour guides, it dawned on me that military organizations have been evolving over thousands of years, but corporations have been doing it for only a few hundred years.

If you go back to the citizen farmer, citizen soldier examples, the Greek phalanx consisted of tight, disciplined units of the Grecian hoplite (citizen farmer) soldiers. The Roman legions led by centurions, the backbone of Roman power, were divided into cohorts. The Mongols created another advanced military organizational model for the time. They based their system on the need to be swift and agile, creating a mobile structure around the decimal system. They divided their units into tens, hundreds, and thousands and could move and reassign units as battles evolved in real time. The evolution of the military structures continued to progress through the centuries, with the Welsh longbowmen organizing themselves in structures close to modern-day battalions. The battalion emerged as the most practical subdivision for larger European armies.

The concept of a battalion dates back to the sixteenth century in Europe from the Italian word *battaglione*, which meant a large body of troops, a formation within larger regiments used to make maneuvering on the battlefield easier.

By the eighteenth century, battalions became better defined as tactical units. European armies created regiments, a collection of two or more battalions. Each battalion functioned as an independent fighting unit.

Under Napoleon, the battalion was further solidified as an essential component of his *corps d'armée* system. French battalions consisted of several companies, including fusiliers, grenadiers, and voltigeurs.

COMBAT ORGANIZATION

This structure influenced many other European armies, including his rivals across the English Channel.

In the British Army, battalions were the building blocks of their military organizational structure. British infantry regiments often comprised two battalions: one serving abroad and the other staying at home. During World Wars I and II, the concept of battalions played a crucial role. While the British didn't invent the battalion, they were instrumental in standardizing and refining its role within military organizations. They were the primary fighting units, often forming part of larger brigades and divisions. The size and structure of battalions varied significantly depending on the nation and the specific requirements of the conflict.

After World War II, many armies restructured their forces with the advent of mechanized warfare and the increased use of technology. Modern battalions often include a mix of infantry, armor, and support elements. Think force multiplication.

Today, battalions are still key tactical units in many armies and are often highly specialized. Each is tailored to a specific combat or support role, and the structure is now reasonably similar across Western nations. The smallest unit is the *squad*, made up of eight to twelve soldiers. Then, two to four squads are combined into a *platoon*. Four platoons make a *company*, four companies make a *battalion*, and four battalions make a *brigade*. The specific number of pieces can vary slightly depending on the branch of service, and pieces can be removed and reassigned depending on the need.

Soldiers are trained to operate within their specific unit. The higher the level, the more complex the mission and the greater the resources available.

At each level, the decision-making process involves gathering information, analyzing the situation, assessing available resources, and determining the best course of action. Decisions are made based on mission objectives, available resources, and the commander's intent.

I was coaching a new director of marketing recently, and we were working on reorganizing their team. As we solidified the pieces, they commented that they would "get with HR to write the job descriptions and post on job boards." How would HR know about your innovative organizational changes and potentially new roles?

Most small- and medium-size businesses won't have dedicated recruiters who specialize. You'll be the only one with expert knowledge of your planned organization and its roles. Don't risk your success by handing off a key component like organizing and hiring.

Most HR professionals I have worked with appreciate the guidance. They will be able to format, confirm salary ranges, and start identifying the right platforms to source the best candidates. At the end of the day, you were chosen to execute a mission and achieve a goal, so don't outsource a key component like hiring.

Standardization Allows Commanders to Move the Pieces on the Board Quickly

Many marketing teams lack the structure that allows a company to be nimble and agile and respond quickly to marketing or business opportunities. Our small- and medium-size businesses have evolved over time and grew during business cycles that allowed for growth, sometimes unevenly. No one sat down at the beginning when there was little revenue and laid out a plan for how the team should look and operate many quarters into the future. The marketing organization was a combination of who was available and what holes we could fill at that moment in time.

This kind of structural design is critical to leading a larger marketing effort. What can you learn from other marketing organizations, even outside your industry?

I created a social movement called Heroes in Recovery at Foundations Recovery Network. Heroes was designed to share stories of recovery and activate our alumni in their communities. Part of the marketing and the kickstart of the movement were 6K runs/walks. We hosted these events in twelve cities. These events were designed to foster conversations around addiction in an effort to mitigate the stigma around openly talking about recovery from substance abuse.

As we built the internal marketing team at Foundations, I studied marketing agencies for insight into organizing our internal marketing team. One of the positions we needed was a coordinator or project manager for all the assets and requests we were busy building through our force multiplication strategy. Agencies I met with all seemed to have a "traffic manager" to handle the inbound and outbound marketing requests, so I added that position to our team. I wrote the job description and partnered with our VP of human resources, Carol Arrowood, to create this new position for the team. We hired Melanie Melcher as our first traffic manager, and our internal team was now better prepared to respond to our rapid growth.

As we consummated our acquisition by Universal Health Services (UHS), our CFO departed, and we were assigned a new person. In one of our first senior team staff meetings, I was caught off guard when our CFO announced that he had analyzed our marketing spend and was recommending immediate changes.

He said we were wasting money by having a full-time person direct automobile and pedestrian traffic at our Heroes 6K runs/walks. Confused, I responded that we don't have a full-time staff member handling such a thing. He showed me our staffing plan document with our "traffic manager" highlighted in yellow. I can't remember who laughed first, but our CEO, Rob Waggener, definitely laughed the loudest.

The takeaway from this funny misunderstanding is this: You will encounter cognitive biases along the way. Make sure you are the organizational expert for your area. Build your knowledge from the front lines. Educate your chain of command so that when a grenade is lobbed your team's way, your leader can support you before you even have a chance to duck.

That was the end of that discussion that morning. It reinforced how important it is to educate and partner with your senior team members. They need to advocate for your organization and know your commander's intent as well.

Organization Is Difficult but Crucial

Organizing your marketing team can be daunting. Early success could have led to uneven growth on your team, and planning for future resources in new technologies or areas can make it hard to socialize internally.

Over the last decade, many companies have been stuck with staff who support declining marketing channels like traditional print, Yellow Pages, television, and radio. Many tried unsuccessfully to repurpose. Can you teach an old dog new tricks? A copywriter for Yellow Pages or radio jingles may not transition to SEO writing. Someone writing for SEO ten years ago is facing a new SEO approach now, not to mention the impact of artificial intelligence. The key is to decide; don't just accept what you have been given if it's not working.

When organizing your marketing operation, numerous models exist from which to learn.

Functional Teams
- Content: Writers and Editors
- Programming/Engineering: Web Developers, Network Administrators, Online Security
- Branding: Graphic Design, Public Relations, UX Design
- Video/Audio: Videographers, Podcasters

Product Based
- Detox Centers
- Residential Centers
- Outpatient Centers
- Surgery Centers
- Dental Practices

Geographical
- All Facilities in the Southeast
- All Dealerships in the Northwest
- By Country
- By State

Integrated/Matrix
- Marketing Resources Assigned to the Automotive Division
- Marketing Resources Assigned to the Manufacturing Plant

COMBAT ORGANIZATION

Segment
- Health Care
- Banking

All have their pros and cons. Integrated marketing allows your forces to align with the business owner, but they could lose continuity with best practices and enterprise leverage.

A geographical structure could align with regional differences in marketing and lower travel costs but create communications challenges.

A product-based structure can allow deep domain expertise but allow siloing to creep in.

Functional marketing allows expertise growth among marketing responsibilities, but does it stay connected to the business?

You have been selected for your position. Choose your structure and implement it. Gather intelligence and seek feedback from both inside and outside your organization. Observe other industries and research whether you can take elements of the best and implement them in your industry.

The military organization is often regarded as one of the most successful organizational models due to its ability to operate efficiently under extreme conditions, adapt to changing situations, and achieve complex objectives.

★

The art of war is like everything else that is beautiful and simple. The simplest moves are the best.
—*Napoleon Bonaparte*[80]

★

Pick a Model That Adapts to Your Changing Needs

No matter your marketing organizational model, will it adapt to changing business needs? Can it succeed in a complicated business environment? How will the team handle disruptive technologies that can upend marketing approaches?

These are core competencies to align your marketing infrastructure with successful military organizations:

1. A clear structure, a defined chain of command, and defined roles and responsibilities facilitate quick decision-making. If you have committees reviewing everything or multiple departments or locations needing to approve items that are your responsibility, you will be delayed and more easily disrupted by competitors.
2. Demanding training creates a culture of excellence.
3. A mission-centric, common goal develops unity of purpose and common efforts among the team.
4. If you're in organizational leadership, you must develop a deep bench of talent and give your commander's intent. Cross-train your team

members and encourage them to accept stretch assignments. This will help you deepen your team's talent.
5. Actively promote team over personal gain. Encourage direct reports to participate in presentations and briefings, even to committees or boards. Showcase the system and team you have built and are leading instead of standing alone on every stage.
6. Encourage and reward creative solutions.

★

Eagles don't flock. You have to find them one at a time.
—Ross Perot[81]

★

Don't Just Take What You Have Been Given

If you don't like the staffing model you have inherited, don't continue with the bad practice. The army doesn't approach it that way.

One of my consulting clients in the Southeast reached out after I had been working with them for a few weeks.

"Lee, I'm preparing to go into an annual review with one of my admissions counselors. She's been there a year. I'm nervous about doing this annual review with her."

"Okay, what were her goals?" I asked.

"Oh, I didn't receive her goals when they hired me six months ago," they replied.

"Well, what are you reviewing?"

You are in command. You will have a honeymoon period from a few weeks to maybe a few months. This is your time to analyze and reorganize, reset, and/or fix the structure of your team. Don't miss out on the chance. Once you have been there for six months, you own the organizational setup, whether you inherited it or not.

---★---

Never tell people how to do things. Tell them what to do and they will surprise you with their ingenuity.
—Gen. George S. Patton[82]

---★---

Lead from the Front and Build Morale

Surveying your situation from the front lines is key. You cannot lead from a bunker in the rear echelon, and you cannot lead from an office with the door closed. This doesn't mean you spend all your time at the front, but you need to be familiar with the actions at the front, and your team needs to not be surprised you are there.

During the American Revolution, George Washington stayed with his men in the encampment at Valley Forge, sharing their hardships at a crucial moment when morale was low. This act of solidarity earned the

COMBAT ORGANIZATION

respect and loyalty of the troops. Being at the front allowed Washington to personally help secure needed food, clothing, and ammunition from Congress and local citizens, alleviating some of the soldiers' immediate physical suffering. His personal engagement reminded the troops of their larger cause. This renewed their shared sense of purpose and fostered a sense of brotherhood and community for his soldiers.

By the end of the winter, the Continental Army emerged as a more disciplined and cohesive force. The improved morale led to significant improvements on the battlefield. Your presence among the team does more than you realize.

As you have organized or reorganized the team and the structure, your personal approach to the building process comes into focus. For many small- and medium-size companies that do not have access to systems like ADP (Automatic Data Processing Inc.), it can be a challenge to systematize and document staff progression, training, and awards. If you don't systematize your process for recognizing achievement and documenting training, all the reorganization you diligently executed will go to waste.

★

People work for money but go the extra mile for recognition, praise, and rewards.
—Dale Carnegie[83]

★

In the county where I live in Middle Tennessee, I volunteer for our Veterans Treatment Court, an alternative sentencing program for veterans. Our volunteer coordinator and one of the founders of our court is Ted Scalise, an Air Force veteran. Ted always wears a baseball-style hat with "DD214" emblazoned on the front, and if you know, you know. It's a fun signal to those who served that Ted's a veteran.

The DD (Defense Department) Form 214, also known as the Certificate of Release or Discharge from Active Duty, is a critical document for the US military. It serves as an official record of a service member's time in the military and includes key information about their service. The form is divided into several sections, each detailing different aspects of the service member's military career.

Two sections, or blocks, of the form are especially important. Block 13 includes decorations, medals, badges, citations, and campaign ribbons awarded or authorized. Block 14 details the soldier's military education. It's like the HR record for the military.

★

Leadership is the art of getting people to do what you want them to do because they want to do it.
—Gen. Dwight D. Eisenhower[84]

★

For many companies, tracking employees' achievements and training often consists of their job description, résumé, and mandatory compliance training. Human resources will not always know your department's strategy or have the software to track certifications, training specific to your team, awards, or special recognition specific to your team.

I am still surprised when I go on-site during an acquisition or a consulting project and learn that the personnel responsible for certain areas are not trained or certified. An example is team members running paid search who are not Google Ads certified. Maybe they were successful in other areas and picked up that assignment, and their leader didn't even know that certifications were readily available. But that's no excuse. If you're leading professionals, you need to educate yourself on what training opportunities and certifications are available to them—especially the credentials other professionals in that field would expect them to have.

Having a system, like your own version of a DD214, will support building a culture that seeks opportunities on its own to grow. That culture will support and recognize training outside the company, speaking engagements at conferences, hosting association events on-site to learn from community experts, and so on. The culture will drive your staff to pursue these opportunities to keep your team at the front versus getting run over from the rear.

I secured a spot at Perot Systems after working with Ross Perot's 1996 presidential campaign. I took full advantage of the robust internal training, including project management training, which included sitting for the Project Management Professional certification. No one had to ask me twice. My billable rate must have increased when I passed. Earning internal and external certifications benefits the company, the customer, and the employee.

These types of opportunities reminded me of the regular opportunities to earn badges and ribbons in the military. Awarding army badges is a process that recognizes and honors the achievements, skills, and

COMBAT ORGANIZATION

dedication of soldiers in various fields. There are three main types of army badges. Combat badges such as the Combat Infantryman Badge (CIB) and Combat Action Badge (CAB) are awarded for direct participation in combat operations. The second type is skill badges such as the Expert Infantryman Badge (EIB), the Air Assault Badge, and the Parachutist Badge. These are awarded for proficiency in specific military skills. The third type is qualification badges, which include Marksmanship and Physical Fitness badges.

Once you meet the eligibility criteria for each badge, your chain of command will start the recommendation process. The soldier's immediate superior will typically recommend the award and document their eligibility. After the badge is approved, a ceremony is often held to present the awarded badge. These ceremonies can be part of a larger event, such as a graduation ceremony or during a unit recognition or promotion event. As these badges are awarded, they are documented in the official military record and eventually make their way to the DD214. Hence why the DD214 holds such importance. Once the badge is awarded, they are worn on their uniforms according to regulations. Each badge represents a significant achievement and is a source of pride for the soldier, reflecting their dedication and expertise in their military career.

These types of awards and recognition ceremonies are rare in the corporate world. When I joined the

Perot Systems recruiting team after my stint on the Perot campaigns, I created my own awards or badges. After my first year on the team, I found a company that could carve anything into the barrel of a baseball bat. I thought that would be a cool award to celebrate the end-of-year recruiting numbers. I had bats carved with the Perot Systems logo for each of my team members, and the middle of the bat was stamped with the number of new hires they had for the year. We continued the tradition the following year with team plaques, and the team-building effects were immeasurable.

Militaries didn't start giving out awards and badges because they needed something to fill up time. Awards and badges recognize personal and group achievements, encouraging a culture of excellence and rewarding exemplary performance. The boost to morale cannot be overstated; recognition reinforces the value of their efforts and contributions to the mission and overall military objectives.

Money can go only so far; acknowledging team members' efforts can lead to higher performance, job satisfaction, team dedication, and employee retention. That last point is just as important in the military as it is in your company. Every time you lose a well-trained employee, you're losing all the experience, expertise, and education you've invested in that person. You can save yourself and your company from these staggering losses simply by being more intentional about how you

COMBAT ORGANIZATION

recognize and reward your team members for their good work.

Esprit de corps, or a shared sense of pride, is especially important, and fostering unit or team pride can strengthen the camaraderie among team members. Awards can highlight team goals and values while aligning with the broader mission. When you arrive at your company, you can always create a basic award opportunity if you don't see a program in place. Document the awards and specialized training your team members succeed in with your human resources team. Even basic certifications like Google Analytics 1 should be documented in their personnel file. Create a culture and watch the esprit de corps grow among your team.

The only guarantee in life and business is your potential. You have everything in front of you, not the least of which is thousands of years of leadership and strategy lessons to apply. Our challenges today are not that far removed from the Greeks, the Carthaginians, and the Romans. In fact, I keep on my nightstand an 1895 copy of Caesar's commentaries on the Gallic War. When people ask me what's the latest marketing book I've come across, I reply, *"Caesar's Commentaries."*

WHAT NEXT?

 Apply this with your team.

How would you reorganize your team?

What best practices do other teams in your industry or marketing agencies use to structure their staff? Your current staff may have some ideas for you based on their backgrounds.

 Apply this with your C-suite.

Present the new structure.

Emphasize how this structure improves the bottom line by enhancing communication, speeding delivery, and helping mirror professional marketing organizations that will yield better retention of your team.

 Gain a quick win.

Document with your human resources department when your staff completes training or certifications.

Host a congratulatory party! Invite your CEO to make the announcement. Could you include it in your corporate newsletter?

Afterword

BE ACTION-ORIENTED TODAY

--- ★ ---

You don't make progress by standing on the sidelines, whimpering and complaining. You make progress by implementing ideas.
—*Shirley Chisholm*[85]

--- ★ ---

Here's what to do next.

What chapter or model spoke to you the most? Apply that to a marketing challenge you have or a strategy you are building. Present your ideas within the context of that model to your leadership or board and be ready to implement them as you break down those barriers to your marketing initiatives.

AFTERWORD

It took me a lifetime to hone these strategies and mental models in my marketing, leadership, and business approach. It is my honor to share them with you.

If this works for you, will you do me a favor?

Will you share the book with a member of your team or someone in your circle of influence who needs to hear this message?

ACKNOWLEDGMENTS

I trust that my family, former coworkers, volunteers, classmates, and army buddies will recognize how this work has evolved and would not have been possible without their support at important times in my life.

I kept this work close to the vest as I started and stopped many times over the last few years. I wish I could have shared it with my father, Lt. Col. Bruce Pepper, before he passed, as he encouraged me to follow in his footsteps.

These concepts were in my head as I embarked on a fourteen-year odyssey with Perot-affiliated groups and companies. It was a whirlwind ride from the moment I faxed off the first press release that my roommate Bill Ayers and I were starting a Students for Perot '92 group. Darcy Anderson, Ed Campbell, Russ Verney, Sharon Drakeford, and Ross Perot took a chance on a young political science graduate from the Volunteer State. Perseverance pays off, and Tony Cinello and Mark

ACKNOWLEDGMENTS

Blahnik took me under their wing at Perot Systems and then allowed me the opportunity to further train and grow under Gary Darling in data center leadership. Mike Morris graciously invited me to relocate back home to Tennessee as Perot Systems was expanding to Nashville.

Being back in Nashville eventually led me to digital music, and many of the staff that I still work with today I met at PassAlong, including Cherie Carter, Wendy Lee Nentwig, David Condos, Zander Jones, Audrey Phillips, Rick Franklin, Jeannie Min, Matt Pfeffer, Mark Pfeffer, Dani Edmonson, Skip Franklin, and Jeff Skillen, just to name a few.

At Foundations Recovery Network, our marketing team did fantastic work and just as importantly they were an unstoppable team. Everyone was pulling for each other to accomplish great things. I could not have accomplished many of my ideas without Cherie Carter leading the charge to implement our innovations. Shawn Manis, Jenny Decker, Anna Mckenzie, Caleb McLaughlin, Kim Fuller, Matt King, Kaitlin Pickrel, Chris Foust, Emily Lindsey, Andrea Morrison, Stephne Hanscom, Stephanie Spann, Joey Darby, Melanie Melcher, Emily Lindsey, Danielle Joyce, AJ Moore, K. Anderson, Sabrina Mathis, Joy Bratton, and Heidi Huerta all first heard my "force multiplication" mantra at Foundations. What a great moment in time to put into practice these strategies and to share with a wider audience.

ACKNOWLEDGMENTS

My time at SpecialtyCare and The Meadows allowed me to continue building teams and planting the seeds for great marketing teams, further honing what would become my treatise. Working with Shawn Mallicoat and George Maney at The Meadows allowed me to formalize these concepts from a digital marketing audience to an operations audience.

All my consulting clients now know who Carl von Clausewitz is! I have also continued learning through engagements with Dr. Daniel Amen, Brad Lamm, Ward Blanchard, Jay Crosson, Nick Hayes, Steve Lee, Thomas McCollum, Adam Mclean, and John and Audra West. I hope this book will allow these concepts to reach an even wider audience.

After I heard Geno Church speak in Nashville, members of my Foundations team visited Brains on Fire in Greenville, South Carolina, to kick off formalizing our Heroes in Recovery movement. Robbin Phillips, Alexis Short, and Heather Hough were instrumental in seeing our idea through to fruition.

The recovery community welcomed me with open arms when I joined Foundations. From the moment John Southworth invited me to start attending open twelve-step meetings, my ideas around the transformational nature of our work became more formalized and in focus. I learned from the best, a true master class featuring Brian O'Shea, Dave Smith, Ken Seeley, Eric Mclaughlin, Peter Loeb, Ruth Ann Rigby, Jennifer

ACKNOWLEDGMENTS

Angier, Paige Bottom, Tad and Tami Stringham, Kelly and Roland Reeves, Michael Hornstein, Vito Tassone, Eial Fischman, Bill Mccormick, Christopher O'Shea, Doug Penny, Dan Parrish, Robert Crocker, and Abhilash Patel. All poured into me to approach all situations with respect and without judgment.

I appreciate Wendy Lee Nentwig's review of the early chapters of my work. My conversations with Nigel Green, Mark Silvestro, and Noah benShea helped me move forward at critical times in this process. Anna McKenzie's review of my book proposal was very helpful, and I am excited to join her as an author. Thank you, Taylor Pope, for your last-minute brainstorming on book titles. Thank you, Kaitlin Pickrel, for your continued professional PR guidance. Liam Curley joined my effort and really guided me on reorganizing and expanding my manuscript. Todd Schlosser provided key insight into my cover design and shared important examples as we were nearing the finish line.

As I immersed myself in the publishing world, I found it daunting. Similar to the music business, the book business had really changed. I worked with Rory and AJ Vaden for many years when they revamped our admissions center training at Foundations. I was so thrilled that a decade later I would walk into their office and learn about Mission Driven Press. Thank you Isla Lake and Carolina Groom for your MDP support in this project. The MDP team's work and Jonathan

ACKNOWLEDGMENTS

Merkh's team at Forefront Books made this process enjoyable. I appreciate Jennifer Gingerich keeping me on schedule and the thoughtful and detailed analysis and edit recommendation that Allen Harris brought to my work. I like working with people who care about these concepts as much as I do!

Randy Campbell was one of the first people in Tennessee to recommend me to the Perot '92 campaign, and he has been instrumental all along the way in guiding me with sound financial and business advice that allowed me the space to complete this work.

I also want to thank my fellow mentors in our Veterans Treatment Court in Williamson County, Tennessee. Ted Scalise and Judge Tom Taylor created our county's program that recognizes the service of our veteran community and creates a safety net that allows veterans the chance to get the help and services they need while navigating our justice system. Many counties in the United States offer something similar, and I encourage all veterans to volunteer their time mentoring in these important programs.

My family has watched me through this process and generously allowed me uninterrupted time when I needed it. Thank you to my mom, Kay Pepper; my brothers, Todd and Kip, and their families; and my in-laws, Tom and Shirley Whayne, for their support. If you need a cheerleader, get my sister-in-law, Heather Parks, on your team; she has been so encouraging.

ACKNOWLEDGMENTS

Thank you, Jennifer, for your years of support and devotion not only on this book but on all the crazy campaign activities, the late-night music industry events, and the faraway recovery conferences. To my sons, Miles and Cy, see what a little bit of work each day can accomplish!

ABOUT THE AUTHOR

Lee has leveraged his service in the United States Army and his experience as a staff member on Ross Perot's presidential campaigns to build great teams that solve technology challenges and grow market share.

During his tenure as chief information officer and chief marketing officer at Foundations Recovery Network, the company grew shareholder value sixtyfold, culminating in its acquisition for $350 million by Universal Health Services. Lee also built the internal marketing teams for SpecialtyCare and Meadows Behavioral Healthcare.

Lee graduated from the University of Tennessee and enlisted in the army before attending Air Assault School and Officer Candidate School and eventually serving eight years mainly in the United States Army Reserves as an armor officer. He resides in Tennessee, where he writes and consults on marketing, leadership,

ABOUT THE AUTHOR

and admissions for health-care clients. Lee also serves as a mentor in Veterans Treatment Court.

Lee is available to speak at your next event, or you can work with him through his one-day private intensives for businesses and marketing teams.

You can reach him through
www.NeverOutmatched.com.

NOTES

1. Chris Grosser, Entrepreneur & Speaker," *Power Talks*, hosted by Life is Positive, June 25, 2023, podcast, RSS.com, https://rss.com/podcasts/lbmusic/1012162/.
2. Exact source for this quote is unverified.
3. Kevin Admiral and Demarius Thomas, "The 3 B's of Armor School: Building the Best-Trained, Best-Led, Best-Equipped Troops," Association of the United States Army, January 22, 2021, https://www.ausa.org/articles/3-bs-armor-school-building-best-trained-best-led-best-equipped-troops.
4. Carl von Clausewitz, *On War*, ed. and trans. Michael Howard and Peter Paret (Princeton University Press, 1976), 34.
5. Sun Tzu, *The Art of War*, trans. L. Giles (originally published 5th century BCE; El Paso Norte Press, 2009), chapter 8, https://archive.org/details/the-art-of-war-by-sun-tzu-trans.-by-lionel-giles-m.-a.-1910.
6. *Patton*, directed by F. J. Schaffner (Twentieth Century Fox, 1970).

NOTES

7. Brett McKay and Kate McKay, "The Maxims of General George S. Patton," The Art of Manliness (blog), January 23, 2017, https://www.artofmanliness.com/character/knowledge-of-men/maxims-general-george-s-patton/.
8. Spencer Stuart. (2024, April). Page 1 *CMO Tenure Study 2024: An Expanded View of CMO Tenure and Background.* Spencer Stuart.com. https://www.spencerstuart.com/research-and-insight/cmo-tenure-study-2024-an-expanded-view-of-cmo-tenure-and-background.
9. Noah benShea, personal communication, January 15, 2025.
10. Tony Robbins (@TonyRobbins), "Identify your problems, but give your power and energy to solutions," *X (formerly Twitter)*, October 17, 2018, https://x.com/TonyRobbins/status/1052643381673750528..
11. "Top 10 Joan of Arc Quotes to Ignite Your Inner Warrior," *Blinkist Magazine*, December 7, 2023, https://www.blinkist.com/magazine/posts/top-joan-arc-quotes-ignite-inner-warrior.
12. Noah benShea, personal communication, January 15, 2025.
13. Napoleon Bonaparte, *The Officer's Manual: Napoleon's Maxims of War* (1862; Project Gutenberg, accessed 2025), https://www.gutenberg.org/files/50750/50750-h/50750-h.htm.
14. Colin L. Powell, "Why Leadership Matters in the Department of State," US Department of State, October

NOTES

28, 2003, https://2001-2009.state.gov/secretary/former/powell/remarks/2003/26930.htm.
15. L. Pockell, ed., *The 101 Greatest Business Principles of All Time* (Warner Books, 2004), 45.
16. Oxford Reference, "Helmuth von Moltke 1880–91: Prussian Military Commander," accessed March 15, 2025, https://www.oxfordreference.com/display/10.1093/acref/9780191826719.001.0001/q-oro-ed4-00007547.
17. Elizabeth Dickason, "Remembering Grace M. Hopper: A Legend in Her Own Time," *Naval History and Heritage Command*, November 13, 2020, https://www.history.navy.mil/research/library/bibliographies/hopper-grace-admiral-select-bibliography/remembering-grace-m-hopper-legend-her-own-time.html.
18. Operations FM 100-5 (Department of the Army, 1982). 1–4.
19. Jean Froissart, *The Chronicles of Froissart*, trans. Lord Berners, ed. G. C. Macaulay, vol. 35, pt. 1 of The Harvard Classics (New York: P.F. Collier & Son, 1909–14; Bartleby.com, 2001), https://www.bartleby.com/35/1/.
20. Kristin Derwinski, "3 Things We Can Learn About Transparency from Theranos," *Stewart Leadership*, June 2022, https://stewartleadership.com/3-things-we-can-learn-about-transparency-from-theranos/.
21. "History Timeline: Post-it® Notes," Post-it Brand, accessed March 15, 2025, https://www.post-it.com/3M/en_US/post-it/contact-us/about-us/.

NOTES

22. Badri Narayan, *Women Heroes and Dalit Assertion in North India: Culture, Identity and Politics* (SAGE Publications, 2006), 45.
23. Carl von Clausewitz, *On War*, trans. James John Graham (CreateSpace, 2022), book 1, p. 46.
24. Ross Perot, *My Life & the Principles for Success* (Summit Publishing Group, 1996), 116.
25. "From Thomas Jefferson to John Jay, 23 August 1785," Founders Online, accessed March 15, 2025, https://founders.archives.gov/documents/Jefferson/01-08-02-0333.
26. Foundations Recovery Network, "Lee Pepper Discussing Heroes in Recovery on Channel 5 Plus Side," YouTube video, November 21, 2013, https://www.youtube.com/watch?v=58T9TTz7iEQ.
27. "First Ladies: Influence and Image—Betty Ford," C-SPAN, April 9, 2014, https://www.c-span.org/video/?318841-1/first-ladies-influence-image-betty-ford.
28. "Our People and Teams," Susan G. Komen, February 13, 2025, https://www.komen.org/about-komen/our-people/.
29. Lee Pepper, host, *Recovery Unscripted Podcast*, "Steve Ford at Moments of Change 2017," Foundations Recovery Network, October 25, 2017, https://www.youtube.com/watch?v=J4Yt04gAD-U&t=34s.
30. Shorty Awards, "GE Brings the World to Work with Employee Profile," accessed May 6, 2025, https://shortyawards.com/12th/ge-brings-the-world-to-work-with-employee-profile.

NOTES

31. Howard Schultz, *Onward: How Starbucks Fought for Its Life Without Losing Its Soul* (Rodale Books, 2011), 77.
32. Jim Harter, "The New Challenge of Engaging Younger Workers," Gallup, February 27, 2024, https://www.gallup.com/workplace/610856/new-challenge-engaging-younger-workers.aspx.
33. Kevin Patrick Emery, "Carthaginian Mercenaries: Soldiers of Fortune, Allied Conscripts, and Multi-Ethnic Armies in Antiquity" (student research paper, Student Scholarship Paper 11, 2016), https://digitalcommons.wofford.edu/cgi/viewcontent.cgi?article=1010&context=studentpubs.
34. Frank Olito and Alex Bitter, "Blockbuster: The Rise and Fall of the Movie Rental Store, and What Happened to the Brand," Business Insider, April 24, 2023, https://www.businessinsider.com/rise-and-fall-of-blockbuster.
35. Will Flanagan, "How McDonald's Hatched Redbox and 7 Other Chicago Companies with In-House incubators," ChicagoInno, May 13, 2015, https://www.bizjournals.com/chicago/inno/stories/news/2015/05/13/how-mcdonalds-hatched-redbox-and-7-other-chicago.html.
36. Annalyn Censky, "Blockbuster Files for Bankruptcy," CNN Money, September 23, 2010, https://money.cnn.com/2010/09/23/news/companies/blockbuster_bankruptcy/index.htm.
37. Aidan McCullen, "Better to Fail Conventionally Than Succeed Unconventionally," The Innovation Show, March 21, 2019, https://theinnovationshow.io/

NOTES

better-to-fail-conventionally-than-succeed-unconventionally/.
38. "Google Algorithm Updates," Search Engine Land, August 15, 2024, https://searchengineland.com/library/platforms/google/google-algorithm-updates.
39. *Encyclopaedia Britannica*, "Battle of Austerlitz," January 31, 2025, https://www.britannica.com/event/Battle-of-Austerlitz.
40. Eric Niderost, "Covered in Glory at Leuthen," *Warfare History Network*, January 7, 2019, https://warfarehistorynetwork.com/article/covered-in-glory-at-leuthen/.
41. Carl von Clausewitz, *On War*, trans. James John Graham (CreateSpace, 2022), book 7, p. 384.
42. Carl von Clausewitz, *On War*, trans. James John Graham (CreateSpace, 2022), book 6, p. 230.
43. Wikipedia, "Sand Table," last modified February 22, 2024, https://en.wikipedia.org/wiki/Sand_table.
44. Robert Mosher, "History of Wargaming—Lieutenant von Reisswitz's Kriegsspiel," Armchair Dragoons, May 6, 2021, https://armchairdragoons.com/nineteenth-century-military-war-games-lieutenant-von-reisswitzs-kriegsspiel/.
45. Sun Tzu, *Art of War*, 57.
46. A. J. Porcelli and M. R. Delgado, "Stress and Decision Making: Effects on Valuation, Learning, and Risk-Taking," *Current Opinion in Behavioral Sciences* 14 (April 2017): 33–39, https://doi.org/10.1016/j.cobeha.2016.11.015.

NOTES

47. M. Zetlin, "Blockbuster Could Have Bought Netflix for $50 Million, but the CEO Thought It Was a Joke," Inc., September 20, 2019, https://www.inc.com/minda-zetlin/netflix-blockbuster-meeting-marc-randolph-reed-hastings-john-antioco.html.
48. J. F. Schmitt, *Mastering Tactics: A Tactical Decision Games Workbook* (Marine Corps Association, September 2002), 2, https://www.mca-marines.org/wp-content/uploads/Mastering-Tactics.pdf.
49. VladRacovita English, "SARISSA: The Weapon That Subjugated The Persian Empire!" YouTube video, February 12, 2022, https://www.youtube.com/watch?v=6MIUD4o-hzk.
50. Richard A. Gabriel, "The Genius of Philip II," HistoryNet, April 4, 2018, https://www.historynet.com/genius-philip-ii/.
51. Johann Wolfgang von Goethe, *Wilhelm Meister's Apprenticeship and Travels*, vol. 1 (of 2) (Project Gutenberg, 2011), https://www.gutenberg.org/ebooks/36483.
52. H. N. Schwarzkopf, with Peter Petre, *It Doesn't Take a Hero: The Autobiography* (Bantam, 1992), chapter 14.
53. J. Charlton, ed., *The Military Quotation Book: More Than 1,200 of the Best Quotations About War, Leadership, Courage, Victory, and Defeat* (Thomas Dunne, 2002), 60.
54. "Examining Advertising and Marketing Practices Within the Substance Use Treatment Industry," House of Representatives, Subcommittee on Oversight and Investigations, Committee on Energy and Commerce, July 24, 2018, https://docs.house.gov/meetings/IF/

NOTES

IF02/20180724/108592/HHRG-115-IF02-Transcript-20180724.pdf.

55. Andrew Nason, "The Greatest Position Never Seen: The Offensive Line," Bleacher Report, June 1, 2018, https://bleacherreport.com/articles/313291-the-greatest-posistion-never-seen-the-offensive-line.

56. Cassius Dio, "The Revolt of Boudica According to Cassius Dio," trans. J. Jackson, Warwick Classics Network, accessed February 16, 2025, https://warwick.ac.uk/fac/arts/classics/warwickclassicsnetwork/romancoventry/resources/boudica/sources/cassiusdio/.

57. Sun Tzu, *Art of War*, 8.

58. Simon Mainwaring, "Purpose-Driven Branding with Simon Mainwaring," Core Speakers Agency, August 2015, https://coreagency.com/blog-post/looking-to-the-future-of-branding-with-simon-mainwaring/.

59. D. W. Knox, "Some Underlying Principles of Morale," *U.S. Naval Institute Proceedings* 42, no. 166 (1916), https://www.usni.org/magazines/proceedings/1916/november/some-underlying-principles-morale.

60. Seth Godin, "What Every Good Marketer Knows," *Seth's Blog*, May 9, 2005, https://seths.blog/2005/05/what_every_good/.

61. D. H. Petraeus, J. F. Amos, and J. A. Nagl, eds., *The U.S. Army/Marine Corps Counterinsurgency Field Manual* (University of Chicago Press, 2007), 49.

62. "The Siege of Boston," Massachusetts Historical Society, accessed January 16, 2025, https://www.masshist.org/online/siege/index.php.

NOTES

63. *U.S. Government Counterinsurgency Guide* (Bureau of Political-Military Affairs, 2009), https://2009-2017.state.gov/documents/organization/119629.pdf.
64. J. Kruger and D. Dunning, "Unskilled and Unaware of It: How Difficulties in Recognizing One's Own Incompetence Lead to Inflated Self-Assessments," *Journal of Personality and Social Psychology* 77, no. 6 (1999): 1121–34, https://doi.org/10.1037/0022-3514.77.6.1121.
65. Charles Darwin, *The Descent of Man, and Selection in Relation to Sex* (John Murray, 1871), https://darwin-online.org.uk/content/frameset?itemID=F937.1&pageseq=1&viewtype=text.
66. Jeff Skillen, personal communication, December 1, 2024.
67. Jan Willem Honig, "Reappraising Late Medieval Strategy: The Example of the 1415 Agincourt Campaign," *War in History* 19 no. 2 (2012): 123–51, https://www.jstor.org/stable/26098426.
68. Peter Drucker, "Nonprofit Prophet," *The Alliance Analyst*, November 11, 1996.
69. Michael Glover, *The Peninsular War, 1807–1814: A Concise Military History* (1974; Penguin Classic Military History, 2001), 45–335.
70. "GoPro and Red Bull Form Exclusive Global Partnership," GoPro, May 24, 2016, https://investor.gopro.com/press-releases/press-release-details/2016/GoPro-and-Red-Bull-Form-Exclusive-Global-Partnership/default.aspx.

NOTES

71. Spencer Johnson, *Who Moved My Cheese? An Amazing Way to Deal with Change in Your Work and in Your Life* (G. P. Putnam's Sons, 1998).
72. Julius Caesar, *Caesar's Gallic War*, trans. Hamilton and Clark (originally published ca. 50 BCE; David McKay, 1895), 288–300.
73. Caesar, *Caesar's Gallic War*, .
74. "1911 Encyclopaedia Britannica/Fortification and Siegecraft," Wikisource, accessed November 17, 2024, https://en.wikisource.org/wiki/1911_Encyclopædia_Britannica/Fortification_and_Siegecraft.
75. Ludwig Heinrich Dyck, "Islam at Vienna's Gates," Warfare History Network, accessed February 17, 2025, https://warfarehistorynetwork.com/article/1683-battle-of-vienna-what-went-wrong-for-ottoman-empire/.
76. *Patton*, directed by F. J. Schaffner (Twentieth Century Fox, 1970).
77. Dwight D. Eisenhower, remarks at the National Defense Executive Reserve Conference, November 14, 1957, https://www.eisenhowerlibrary.gov/eisenhowers/quotes.
78. Caesar, *Caesar's Gallic War*, 262–84.
79. "Quotes from Philip Kotler," *Philip Kotler Official Website*, 2025, https://www.pkotler.org/quotes-from-pk.
80. *Bartlett's Familiar Quotations*, 18th ed., ed. Geoffrey O'Brien (New York: Little, Brown and Company, 2012).
81. Perot, *My Life*, 135.
82. George S. Patton, Jr., *War As I Knew It*, ed. Paul D. Harkins (Boston: Houghton Mifflin, 1947).

NOTES

83. "Top 10 Quotes About Rewards and Recognition," Awards Network, accessed March 15, 2025, https://blog.awardsnetwork.com/top-10-quotes-rewards-recognition.
84. Dwight D. Eisenhower, remarks at the Annual Conference of the Society for Personnel Administration, May 12, 1954, https://www.eisenhowerlibrary.gov/eisenhowers/quotes.
85. "Celebrating Shirley Chisholm: a Trailblazer, a Change Maker, and Our Inspiration," The Chisholm Legacy Project, November 30, 2023, https://thechisholmlegacy-project.org/celebrating-shirley-chisholm-a-trailblazer-a-change-maker-and-our-inspiration/.
86. Brett McKay and Kate McKay, "The Maxims of General George S. Patton," *The Art of Manliness* (blog), January 23, 2017, https://www.artofmanliness.com/character/knowledge-of-men/maxims-general-george-s-patton/.
87. McKay and McKay, "The Maxims of General George S. Patton."